PURSUING THE PAST

PURSUING THE PAST

ORAL HISTORY
PHOTOGRAPHS
FAMILY HISTORY
CEMETERIES

Eugene F. Provenzo, Jr.
and
Asterie Baker Provenzo

Design: Peter A. Zorn, Jr.

Addison-Wesley Publishing Company
Menlo Park, California • Reading, Massachusetts
London • Amsterdam • Don Mills, Ontario • Sydney

PURSUING THE PAST is in two volumes. Volume II contains
the following chapters:

- Maps and Mapping
- City and Neighborhood
- Architecture
- The World of Work

Volume II Student Edition (5 copies): Order code 20130
Volume II Teacher's Edition (1 copy) and Student Edition (1 copy): Order code 20126

This book was written on an Apple II microcomputer. The final text was transmitted by a Hayes Micromodem to Supertype, Inc., Hialeah, Florida, where type proofs were generated on a Mergenthaler Phototypesetter. The text of the book was set in 12 point Garamond Light. Final design and preparation of camera-ready copy was completed by Peter A. Zorn, Jr. and the authors in Miami, Florida. Editorial review, printing, and distribution were provided by Addison-Wesley Innovative Division, Menlo Park, California.

This book is published by the ADDISON-WESLEY INNOVATIVE DIVISION. The blackline masters in this publication are designed to be used with appropriate duplicating equipment to reproduce copies for classroom use. Addison-Wesley Publishing Company grants permission to classroom teachers to reproduce these masters.

Copyright © 1984 by Addison-Wesley Publishing Company, Inc. All rights reserved. Printed in the United States of America. Published simultaneously in Canada.

ISBN 0-201-20208-5

7 8 9 10 - ML - 95 94 93 92

Eugene F. Provenzo, Jr., a professor in the School of Education and Allied Professions, University of Miami, is a specialist in the history of childhood and education. He earned an undergraduate degree in history from the University of Rochester, an MA in history and a PhD in the history and philosophy of education from Washington University, St. Louis. He has taught social studies at the secondary level.

Provenzo has written a number of studies on local history including *The History of The St. Louis Car Company* (with Andrew David Young, Howell-North Books, 1978). He has recently written the *History of Education and Culture in America* (with H. Warren Button, Prentice-Hall, Inc., 1983) and *The Complete Block Book* (with Arlene Brett, Syracuse University Press, 1983.)

He is currently working on studies dealing with the sociology of teaching and on the impact of computers on American culture and education.

Asterie Baker Provenzo is a freelance writer. She earned her undergraduate degree in art history and an MA in Asian studies from Washington University in St. Louis, and has done graduate work in architectural history at both Washington University and the University of Miami.

She and her husband collect antiques and family memorabilia, especially toys and board games. As an outgrowth of their research on the history of childhood and education they have written *Play It Again: Board Games From the Past You Can Make and Play Yourself* and *The Historian's Toybox: Children's Toys From the Past You Can Make Yourself* (illustrated by Peter A. Zorn, Jr., Prentice-Hall, Inc., 1981, 1980).

As a consultant she was recently involved in a cooperative museum program between the Historical Museum of Southern Florida and the Dade County schools. The proposed history/museum program, "Florida Explorer," will involve all of the county's fourth-grade students.

Peter A. Zorn, Jr. is an associate professor in Graphic Design and Illustration, University of Miami. He earned a BFA from the Cleveland Institute of Art and an MFA from the University of Miami.

Zorn lives with his wife and young daughter in an 1896 Florida farmhouse that they are restoring. He collects antique guns and automobiles and builds exact scale models of vintage automobiles and aircraft. Four of his paper model airplane books have been published: *Fokker Dr. 1 Triplanes; Spad XIII and Spad VII; Ford Trimotor 5-AT;* and *Spirit of St. Louis Ryan NYP* (with Eugene and Asterie Provenzo, Crown Publishers, Inc., 1982).

For Eugene F. Provenzo, Sr.
History teacher, parent, and friend

ACKNOWLEDGMENTS

Many different people and organizations have contributed to the writing of *Pursuing the Past*. A summer fellowship from the Newberry Library in Chicago, funded by the National Endowment for the Humanities in 1978, allowed the authors to begin the research and writing for the project. We wish to especially thank Richard H. Brown, Director of Research and Education at the Newberry, for his interest in the project and critical suggestions. Richard Jenson, D'Ann Campbell, and the staff of the Family and Community History Center at the Newberry also provided us with important support.

While we were working in Chicago, Glen Holt gave us many helpful suggestions on finding resources in the Chicago and St. Louis areas. His knowledge of local historical resources and his research on both St. Louis and Chicago history have provided us with important insights into the nature of family and commmunity history.

In 1976 and 1977, one of the authors participated in the development of a local history curriculum for the St. Louis area. Sponsored by the National Endowment for the Humanities under the direction of the Central Midwestern Regional Educational Laboratory (CEMREL), the project represented the beginning of our work in local, family, and community history. We would like to thank Marilyn Mann and Betty Hall in particular, for all of their help with our work at CEMREL. Many of our ideas for *Pursuing the Past* originated in our discussions with them.

In Miami, we wish to thank some of our colleagues at the School of Education and Allied Professions, University of Miami — Arnold Cheyney, Maria Llabre, Charles Hanneman, and Scott Baldwin — for their thoughtful suggestions. Helen Biebel, Mildred Merrick, Sara Sanchez, and Lesbia Varona of the Otto G. Richter Library, University of Miami, always answered our questions and helped make our research in the library a pleasant experience. Becky Smith and Randy Nimnicht of the Historical Association of Southern Florida have also been generous with their help. Aubrey Simms was kind enough to lend us materials from her family photographic collection. Julia Thrane Zorn helped us with photographic work and also lent us some of her family photographs. Peter A. Zorn, Jr., our designer, illustrator, and friend deserves special recognition as a creative contributor to both this and so many of our other projects.

We would like to thank the Innovative Division of Addison-Wesley for its interest in our work and thoughtful contributions to it.

Finally, we would like to thank some of the members of our family for their generous help and their contributions to *Pursuing the Past*: Eugene F. Provenzo, Sr., Therese M. Provenzo, Ann T. Freedman, Steven D. Freedman, Elizabeth (Shep) Sporel, Camille Provenzo Fiorella, Asterie S. Baker, Grace H. Schultz, Maia Floris Schultz, David F. Baker, Charles D. Baker, and Marguarete Martin Bowers.

TABLE OF CONTENTS

PAGE

INTRODUCTION
1

Chapter 1: ORAL HISTORY
5

Collecting Oral History — 8
Hints For Conducting an Oral History Interview — 8
More Hints For Conducting an Oral History Interview — 9
After the Interview — 10
Stretching the Truth in Oral History Interviews — 12
Checking the Accuracy of Oral History Interviews — 15
Different Types of Oral History Interviews — 16
The Value of Oral History Interviews — 19

Chapter 2: PHOTOGRAPHS
23

How to Analyze and Identify Photographs — 28
Different Types of Historical Information to
  be Found in Photographs — 29
Comparing Historical Photographs For More Information — 34
How to Fill Out a Photograph Analysis Chart — 37
Faked and Altered Photographs — 46
How to Handle Photographs as Historical Documents — 50
Photocopying Photographs — 50
Types of Photographs and Photographic Processes — 51

Chapter 3: FAMILY HISTORY   55

Sources of Family History   64
Tracking Down Family Stories   68
Names Tell Stories Too   74
Using Archives, Libraries, and Government
    Records to Trace Your Family's History   78
Using Birth, Marriage, and Death Certificates
    to Trace Your Family's History   80
Using the Federal Census Records to Trace Your
    Family's History   80
Using Passenger Arrival Lists to Trace Your
    Family's History   81
Useful Terms In Studying Family History And Genealogy   82

Chapter 4: CEMETERIES   87

Different Types Of Cemeteries   90
Visiting Cemeteries   93
Sources Of Historical Information In Cemeteries   95
A Walk Through History   99
How to Read Inscriptions   99
Epitaphs: Messages From the Dead   102
Symbolism Found on Tombstones and Monuments   104
Preserving Cemeteries and Their History   109
How to Make a Rubbing   110
Useful Terms in Studying Cemeteries   113

INTRODUCTION

Pursuing the Past: Oral History, Photographs, Family History, And Cemeteries is not a history textbook. It is a book about how to discover the past for yourself. You will learn how to use the different types of evidence that surround you in your family and community to think about, investigate, and record history. You will learn what a historian does and how to be one yourself.

Every person (including you), every family, and every community has always been a part of something much larger. By taking a closer look at your family and community you will discover how people close to you have participated in the history of our country and the world. At the same time you will discover how large, historical events have affected the history of your community and family — even your own history.

By investigating the history of your family and community you will be able to use many different kinds of firsthand evidence. This evidence can be found:

In your own memory and the memories of your friends and relatives.

In the photographs in your family album.

In the pages of a family Bible.

In one of the local cemeteries.

Firsthand evidence is from the original source. Any evidence that is original is considered to be "primary" evidence. Therefore, a *primary source* is a direct record left behind about a person, an object, or an event. Historians like to use primary or original sources because they provide clues to the past that haven't been tampered with or reconstructed.

(Telegram: Courtesy The Library of Congress. Letters: Courtesy Smithsonian Institution.)

Throughout *Pursuing the Past*, you will have many opportunities to investigate primary sources. In fact, one of the advantages of investigating the history of your family and community is that you have so many primary sources close at hand. Letters, diaries, photographs, buildings, and personal memories are all primary sources. In learning how to use these different types of evidence, you will also learn how to analyze and interpret the evidence. For example, you will learn that photographs may not always be what they seem. A photograph of an event can be tampered with. However, if you combine the photograph with other types of evidence such as a personal reminiscence or letter describing the event, you will have a better chance of discovering what really happened.

A newspaper account of an event is another type of evidence. It is not original and therefore is secondhand evidence. Newspaper articles, magazine articles, and books are usually reconstructed evidence, or *secondary sources*. However, if these accounts have been created by someone who actually took part in the event, they are considered a primary source of evidence.

For example, a book describing the Wright Brothers' discovery of flight would be a secondary source. However, a letter written by Orville or Wilbur Wright describing their work would be a primary source. Likewise, an unretouched photograph of them flying would be a primary source of historical information.

In *Pursuing the Past* you can learn how to use primary sources from your own family and community, as well as secondary sources, to pursue the past. You can learn how to use this evidence to solve the mysteries of past events and to discover how people's experiences were both different and similar to your own. You may even discover how the past has influenced the present and is in fact present in your day-to-day life. We hope you discover that history is a lot more interesting, and that being a historian is a lot more fun, than you ever suspected.

(Courtesy Smithsonian Institution.)

INTERVIEWEE: Chief Red-Horse (Sioux)

SUBJECT: Red Horse's memories of "Custer's Massacre"

INTERVIEWER: Charles E. McChesney, Acting Assistant Surgeon

Location: Cheyenne River Agency, South Dakota

Date: 1881

Here follows the story of Red-Horse:

Five springs, ago I, with many Sioux Indians, took down and moved from Cheyenne river to the Rosebud river, where we then took down and packed up our lodges and moved to the and pitched our lodges with the large camp of Sioux.

The Sioux were camped on the Little Bighorn river as the Uncpapas were pitched highest up the river under lodges were pitched next. The Oglala's lodges were p lodges were pitched next. The Minneconjou lodges were Arcs' lodges were pitched next. The Blackfeet lodges Cheyenne lodges were pitched next. A few Arikara In (being without lodges of their own.) Two-Kettles, a (without lodges).

I was a Sioux chief in the council lodge. My lodge of the camp. The day of the attack I and four wome the camp digging wild turnips. Suddenly one of the attention to a cloud of dust rising a short dista that the soldiers were charging the camp. To the When I arrived a son told me to hurry to the charged so q could not talk (council). lodge and en and children mount ho fight

officer who rode a h his officer was Cap me fought many br the bravest m er or not. Man his officer i ld me that h wore a lar f many soldie say this office alike.

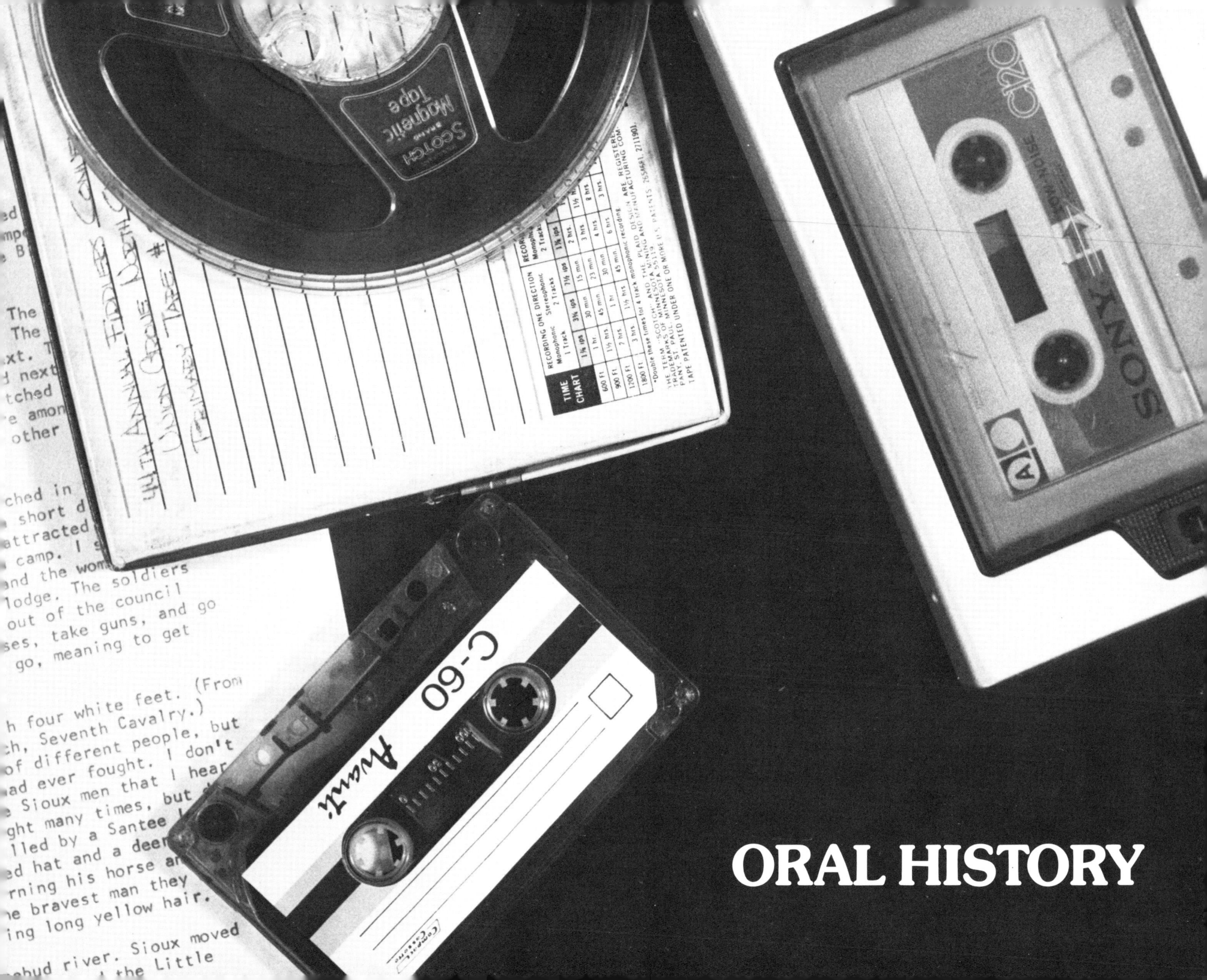

ORAL HISTORY

Chapter 1: ORAL HISTORY

Modern historians tend to pay more attention to written and printed sources of history than to oral sources. Yet history has not always depended upon the written word. In most ancient cultures, historical information was transmitted from one generation to the next by means of the spoken word. This tradition of oral history can still be found today in the folk traditions of many different cultures.

Since the 1950s and the introduction of inexpensive tape recorders, oral history has become increasingly popular. With its growing use, many new primary sources of historical information and firsthand accounts of historical events have been discovered.

Oral history is both exciting and difficult. It demands that you not only listen carefully, but also ask the right questions. A good oral history interview should have a specific purpose. Almost everyone has interesting stories about experiences they have had and people they have known. Such stories are of little historical value, however, unless they are put into a specific context. However, by doing an oral history interview, you are actually helping to create an historical record.

People's memories can help us discover and better understand people who lived before us and the past. Oral history interviews are an important way for us to find out about people who didn't happen to leave diaries, letters, or other written records behind. And as more and more communication takes place over the telephone, leaving no record for the future, oral history will become an even more important tool for discovering the past.

would be able to focus your questions around a theme and really explore it through their memories:

What were your favorite games as a child and how were they played?

How did your parents discipline you as a child?

How did you earn or get money as a child?

Themes and topics that focus on specific events, issues, and people generally work best. You may find it easier to focus your interviews on subjects and issues found in your own family or community.

HINTS FOR CONDUCTING AN ORAL HISTORY INTERVIEW

If you are using a tape recorder, check that it is in good working order. If possible, plug in your recorder, rather than relying on batteries. Always bring more than one tape, and extra batteries. Be sure to change a tape before it runs out.

Practice using the tape recorder before the interview. During the interview make sure that you position the microphone so that it will pick up everything that is being said. It is a good idea to run a voice level test before beginning the interview. In order to get a voice level, turn on the recorder and say something simple like "Testing, 1, 2, 3," and then play it back to decide how high the volume must be to pick up the voice of the person you are interviewing.

COLLECTING ORAL HISTORY

Collecting oral history can be a great deal of fun. It does take a little practice, however, and a bit of planning. Before you begin an interview make sure that you have clearly defined a specific theme or topic for the interview. Don't choose a topic that is too broad.

For example, an oral history interview with one of your grandparents about his or her childhood would be too broad a topic. However, if you chose one of the following topics for an interview with them, you

If you are taking notes rather than recording an interview, don't try to record every word. Write down key words and phrases. Use abbreviations. Extensive note-taking tends to distract the person being interviewed. After the interview is over, you can go back over your notes and fill in the blanks. Make sure you do this as soon as possible after the interview, while your memory is still fresh.

Always identify the person you are interviewing, the date, and the location of the interview at the beginning of your recording or notes.

Try to make the person you are interviewing as comfortable as possible. It may help to conduct the interview in the person's home. Pick a spot where they are most comfortable, such as at the kitchen table or in a den. Choose a time for the interview when you are not likely to be interrupted. Talking informally for a few minutes before the interview is often helpful.

YOUR BIRTHDAY AS HISTORY

Now that you have learned some of the important points about oral history interviews, why not practice them by conducting a few simple, short interviews. The subject will be yourself. You will actually be creating a historical record about yourself by talking with members of your family.

Have you ever thought about the day you were born? What happened that day in the world? Were there any important events that took place?

Interview some of the people who were there when you were born. Ask your mother and father what they were doing. Where was your father when he found out you were about to be born? What were your grandparents doing? If you have an older brother or sister, do they remember anything about it? Try to recreate what the day was all about.

Now that you have completed your first oral history interviews, perhaps you can see how oral history can be used to supplement or complement the written records we have about a person, an event, or an issue. Oral history interviews can help you fill in the missing links, the gaps, in the history of your family and community. Throughout the other chapters in *Pursuing the Past* you may often decide that an oral history interview is just the tool you need to try to discover some missing information, or to explain information you don't completely understand.

However, oral history interviews are not easy — especially when you are conducting an interview with someone you don't know or about a topic you know very little about. Let's examine some more hints for conducting interviews.

MORE HINTS FOR CONDUCTING ORAL HISTORY INTERVIEWS

Try to keep on the subject you have chosen for the interview. If the person you are interviewing starts to ramble, subtly ask a question that leads him or her back to the topic.

For example, suppose you are interviewing an older person about what elementary school was like when he was younger. He might begin to talk more about his favorite sports when he was young than about school. You could ask one of the following questions to help bring him back to the subject:

What games did you play during recess periods?

Did you have gym classes?

The questions are related enough to sports that you won't appear to be rudely changing the subject. At the same time you are steering the interview back to the chosen topic.

Be aware of who is doing most of the talking during the interview. Remember that you are interested in learning what the interviewee has to say about your topic. If you do most of the talking you won't learn very much.

Don't hurry through your interview.

If the interviewee responds to questions with only "yes" and "no" answers, ask him or her to elaborate and go into greater detail.

If an answer from an interviewee is unclear or you don't understand part of it, be sure to try to get the person you are interviewing to explain it to you. Don't be afraid to admit that you don't know the meaning of a term he or she uses; the location of a place he or she refers to; or what an object is that he or she is talking about. After all, an oral history interview is supposed to be a learning experience for you, too.

Be careful not to let your own movements or gestures — like a raised eyebrow or a frown — interrupt the person's train of thought.

An oral history interview is an open-ended process. This means that you never know what is going to turn up. You must be flexible. You may want to explore surprises that pop up in the interview.

For example, again suppose that you are interviewing an older person about what elementary school was like when she was young. In response to one of your questions she says:

"I don't have any memories of going to school in the fourth grade."

You might ask, "Why not?" And the person you're interviewing might respond:

"Because my father died and I had to help my mother run the bakery shop that the family owned."

As the interviewer, you may decide to build the rest of your questions about schooling in the past upon this hardship. Was this person ever able to go back to school and complete her education? Did she educate herself? Did she believe that an education was important?

AFTER THE INTERVIEW

Store the tapes you have collected in a safe place, clearly labeling them so that you can easily find them again.

Professional historians almost always transcribe their tapes in order to be able to use data from them more easily. You may wish to do this for your own projects. Accuracy is particularly important when transcribing a tape, since you are also establishing a permanent historical record with the transcript. Transcripts should be labeled and identified the same way as a tape.

WHAT WAS SCHOOL LIKE?

Have you ever wondered what it was like to go to school twenty-five or fifty years ago? Interview your parents, grandparents, or friends of your family to discover what school was like in the past.

What types of subjects were studied? Was discipline the same as it is today? What did students wear to school? How large were classes and who taught them? How did the school building look and smell?

If you go to a school that was built a very long time ago, it might be fun to try to find someone who is older who also went to the school. Compare his or her experiences in the school with your own. How has the school changed? What things are still the same?

STRETCHING THE TRUTH IN ORAL HISTORY INTERVIEWS

There are some problems that may come up when you are doing oral history interviews. Often, when interviewing an individual about a set of events, you will find that he or she forgets an important fact. Or he or she may embellish other facts or stretch the truth a bit. Sometimes when we remember events or places, certain facts are exaggerated in our memories.

This tendency should not be confused with lying. It is natural for people to feel that they played particularly important roles in events when in reality they may have simply been onlookers.

You can easily see how this tendency works with yourself. Think about the house you lived in as a young child. If you were asked to describe it without having seen it for some years, you probably would remember it as being much larger than it actually is.

It isn't as big as I remembered.

LIFE THEN AND NOW

How we conduct our day-to-day lives has changed in subtle ways over the years. Have you ever thought about how kitchens are different today from what they were like for your parents or grandparents when they were children?

Make a diagram of the kitchen in the house or apartment where you live. Include all the appliances such as refrigerators, electric can openers, dishwishers, and so on.

Now ask your parents or grandparents to describe what the kitchens of their homes were like when they were your age. How were they the same and how were they different from today?

How was food stored in the kitchens of your parents and grandparents? What appliances did they have? How were the kitchens used by the family?

What do these comparisons tell you about how day-to-day life has changed?

14

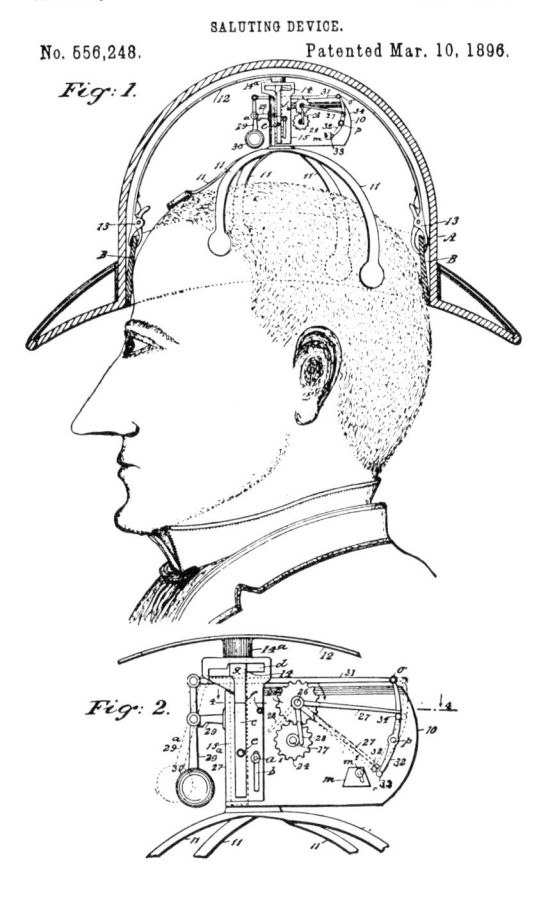

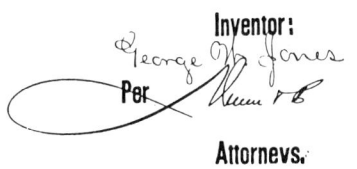

CHECKING THE ACCURACY OF ORAL HISTORY INTERVIEWS

Interviewers collecting oral history often must check the accuracy of the data they are getting from their sources. This can be done in a number of different ways. For example, information can be checked against other written primary sources or secondary sources.

Suppose someone you are interviewing claims to have invented a specific machine. You could look up the patent for the device, which would be a primary source, and see who is given credit for its invention.

Suppose you are trying to discover more about a particular historical event. Interview two different people who witnessed it. Check whether their descriptions of what happened agree with one another and with the available secondary sources of information on the event.

If one source is consistently accurate, it is probably safe for you to trust it about data that are difficult to verify against other sources. If a person has proven to be particularly unreliable, then you should probably treat what he or she says with a high degree of doubt or skepticism.

WITNESSING HISTORY

Your parents, and perhaps even an older brother or sister, have all lived through important historical events. They may remember the first landing on the moon or the assassinations of President John F. Kennedy and Martin Luther King, Jr.

Ask them where they were and what they were doing when these events took place. Do they remember how they felt about these events? Ask them to recall to you as much as they possibly can.

Compare their accounts of these historical events with other secondary sources of information on the event, such as newspaper or magazine accounts.

Do you remember any important historical events that took place when you were younger? What is it that makes these events seem important? Why do they remain as "frozen moments" in your memory?

DIFFERENT TYPES OF ORAL HISTORY INTERVIEWS

Oral history interviews can be conducted with many different types of people and for many different purposes. *Elite* interviewing, for example, involves interviewing well-known or important people about various aspects of their lives and experience. Many examples of this type of oral history interview can be found in the Columbia University Oral History Project. It has tried to focus on interviewing leading statesmen, businessmen, and educators — people who have played important roles in shaping our history and culture.

Non-elite interviewing generally involves gathering information from people who may have had important experiences but probably are not well-known. Examples of this type of interview can be found in Studs Terkel's book *Working*. He explores what life is like for people working in many different types of jobs.

An example of a non-elite oral history interview was conducted by one of the authors at the Maribel Cigar Factory in Miami, Florida. He interviewed exiled and immigrant craftsmen who are carrying on the tradition and craft of making hand-rolled cigars that they learned in Cuba. Not only is their trade an interesting one, but these people may be among the last to know how to hand-roll cigars.

The women and men interviewed were able to describe how they learned their trade and to give detailed instructions on how to roll a fine cigar. Here is part of Jose Gonzalez's story:

Interviewer: What is your name?

Jose: Jose Gonzalez.

Interviewer: How old are you?

Jose: Sixty years old.

Interviewer: When did you come to the United States?

Jose: In 1969.

Interviewer: In Cuba, did you work in the cigar industry?

Jose: In a cigar factory. At the age of thirteen I worked in the selection of tobacco. I performed all the types of work that are performed in the selection of tobacco. Later I learned to be a roller, seeking a stable means of life.

Interviewer: So you really came into the rolling of cigars having been through the complete process of the job.

Jose: Exactly!

Interviewer: How did you learn to roll cigars?

Jose: Well, I went to a small cigar factory. I started looking at what the others did, and as soon as I was given a chance, I started rolling. I made friends with an experienced roller, and he would allow me to roll some. I would spoil some tobacco to learn. After a while, I could roll the cigars.

(Courtesy The Historical Association of Southern Florida.)

SEARS, ROEBUCK & CO., CHICAGO, ILL. CATALOGUE No. 117.

3 No. 1 tins **71c**
No. 7K53083

30-bar box **$1.02**
No. 7K74007

6-lb. box **35c**
No. 7K6705

Both for **75c**
No. 7K4399

6 No. 1 cans **59c**
No. 7K52796

15-lb. pail **$1.00**
No. 7K55207

12,000 matches **58c**
No. 7K79017

5-lb. pkg. **49c**
No. 7K4770

3 1-lb. pkgs. **15c**
No. 7K67113

3 1-lb. pkgs. **12c**
No. 7K42923

1-lb. can **35c**
No. 7K4258

WHAT'S COOKING?

You probably know a lot about your favorite foods. But do you realize that the preparation of food and our eating habits have changed enormously for most Americans in recent years? Prepared and packaged frozen foods, dehydrated foods, and fast food restaurants such as MacDonald's and Burger King are all relatively recent.

An oral history interview with your parents or grandparents on this topic would be a good way to find out about foods in the past. Ask them how their eating habits have changed since they were children. Do they still eat the same foods they did when they were younger? Ask them how prices for food have changed. How much did a candy bar cost, for example, when your parents were children? How much did a bottle of Coca-Cola cost? Can they still find their favorite foods?

You might also ask them how their food was packaged. Did cereal come in boxes? What did old soft drink bottles look like?

THE VALUE OF ORAL HISTORY INTERVIEWS

Perhaps the greatest contribution that oral history as a field has made is to increase our understanding of people who do not leave the traditional written records that historians most often use.

For example, oral history projects have been undertaken with minority groups such as the native Americans or Indians. A great deal of information on the role and treatment of native Americans in our culture has emerged from these interviews. It is information about the past that would otherwise have been lost forever.

A fascinating example of the special information that has survived because of an oral history interview can be found in an interview with the Sioux Indian, Red Horse. Red Horse was a Sioux chief who fought at the Battle of the Little Bighorn, or Custer's Last Stand, in 1876.

Five years after the battle he was

The Sioux Chief, Red Horse. (Courtesy the National Museum of Natural History, Smithsonian Institution.)

"The soldiers charged the Sioux camp about noon. The soldiers were divided, one party charging right into the camp. After driving these soldiers across the river, the Sioux charged the different soldiers [Custer's] below, and drove them in confusion..." From Red Horse's oral history account of the Battle of the Little Bighorn, 1881. Custer's Column Fighting. (Courtesy the National Museum of Natural History, the Smithsonian Institution.)

interviewed about his memories of the day and battle. He used sign language to describe his memories since he could not speak English. Unfortunately, none of the interviewer's questions survive. We only have a transcript, in the form of a monologue, of Red Horse's account of the event.

Red Horse also drew simplified pictures or pictograms of his memories of the event. One of these drawings and a brief segment of his description of the battle are included on the previous page.

Since General Custer and all of his men were killed in the battle, Red Horse's oral history interview is one of the only surviving accounts of the famous battle.

Many factors determine whether or not an oral history interview is successful:

> The attitude and involvement of the interviewee.

> The preparation of the interviewer.

> Whether or not rapport can be established between the interviewer and interviewee.

An oral history interview can be your link to people and their innermost memories, to experiences, and events from the past. Oral history can make the past come alive for you. However, oral history interviews do not always have to be conducted with older people. Even your younger brother's or sister's memories of their first day at school, or of an important national event, are history. Remember, your record of the interviews can become a permanent contribution to history.

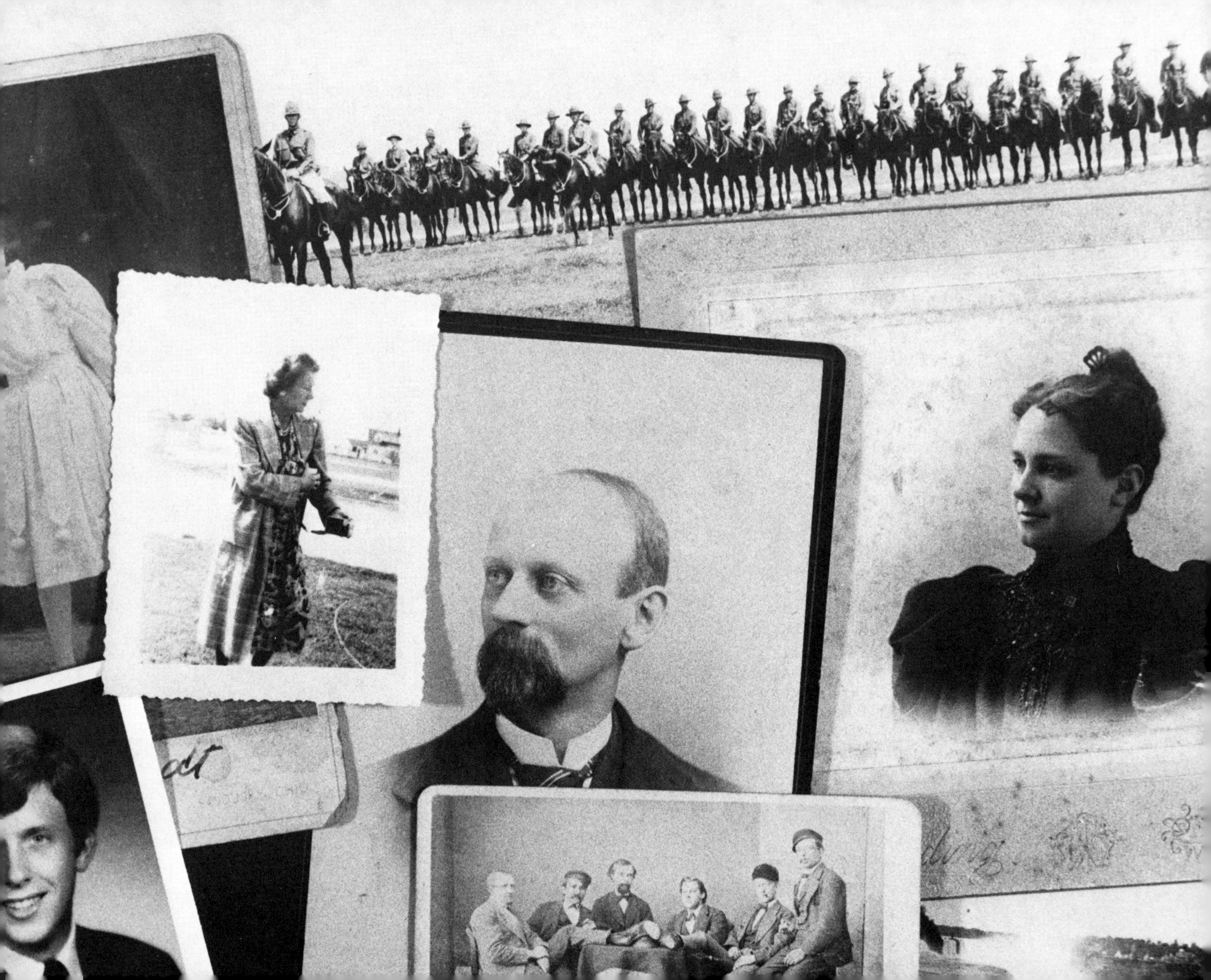

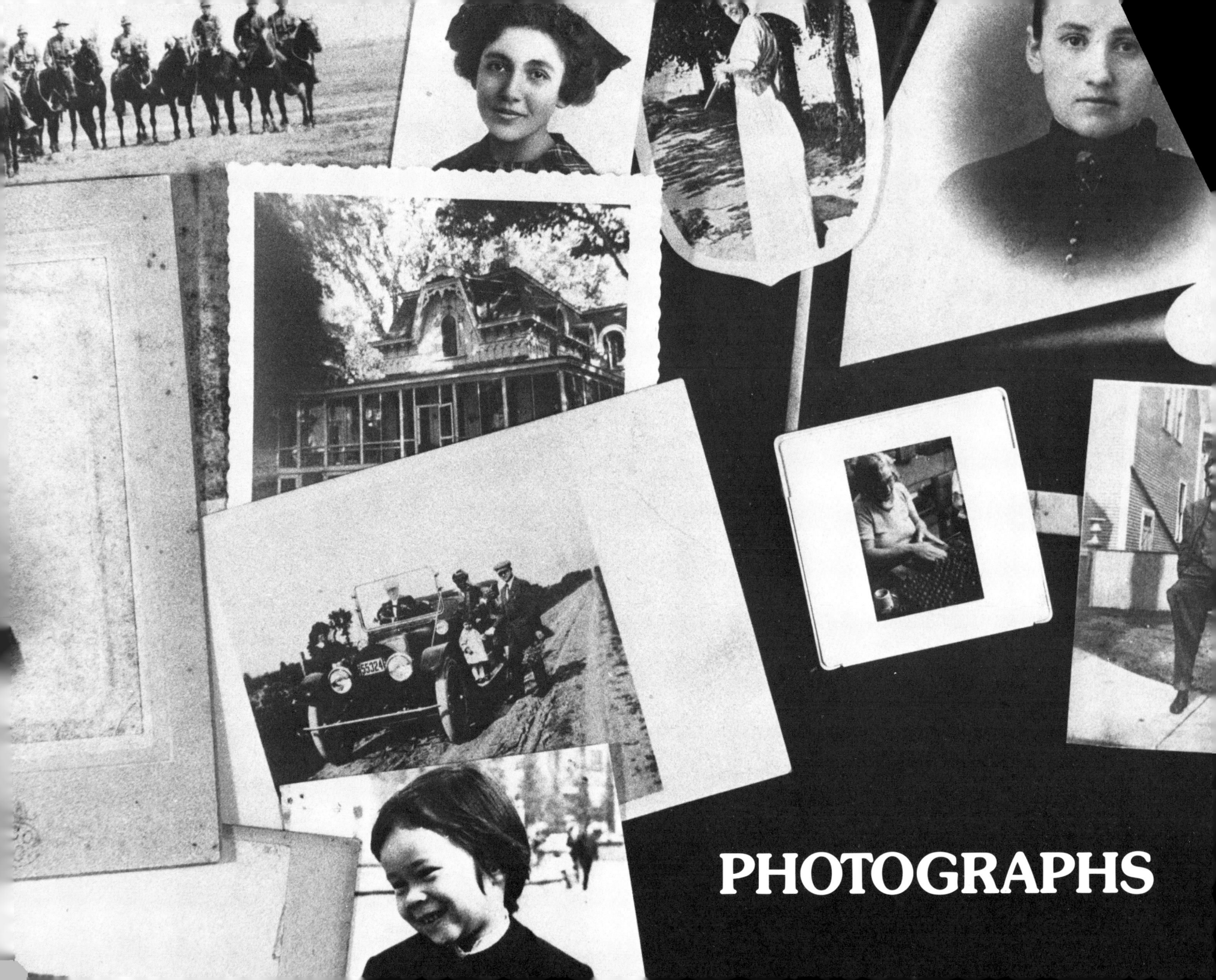

PHOTOGRAPHS

Chapter 2: PHOTOGRAPHS

Since its invention in the early 1800s, photography has provided us with new ways of looking at ourselves and the world. Photographs surround us in magazines, books, and newspapers; on posters, billboards, and television. They are a very important part of our day-to-day lives. Yet, have you ever thought about how photographs can help you discover the past? Photographs are primary sources of historical information that can provide you with direct links to the past.

Nearly every photograph contains some historical information. Photographs tell us important facts about their subjects and about the society in which they were taken. They can also tell us about the people who took them. Photography requires that a person pause and focus on the subject of their photograph. Therefore, taking a photograph is a selective process. By carefully analyzing a photograph, you can often discover something about the interests and viewpoint of the photographer.

Frances B. Johnson. Tintype Studio, about 1890. (Courtesy George Eastman House, Rochester, N.Y.)

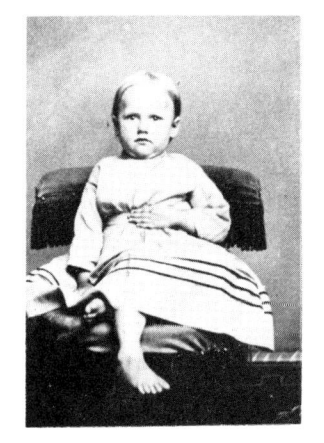

25

INTERPRETING PHOTOGRAPHS

Cut three photographs that interest you out of some old magazines or newspapers. Now imagine that you are an historian some time in the future looking at these pictures. Analyze each picture.

What is the subject of each picture? What is happening in the picture? Why was the photograph probably taken? Do these photographs tell you anything about the viewpoint of the photographer?

What does your analysis of these three photographs tell you about the history and society at the time they were taken? Is your understanding of history limited in some way by the photographs you have chosen to examine? Do they give you a complete picture of an historical period?

Photographs by Michael L. Carlebach

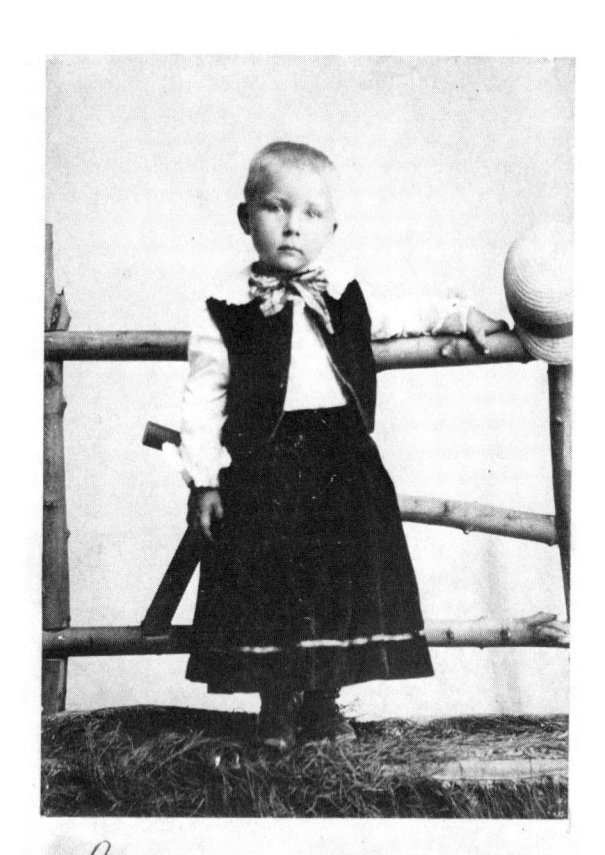

HOW TO ANALYZE AND IDENTIFY PHOTOGRAPHS

Analyzing photographs for what they can tell you about the past takes practice. Where and how a picture was taken can often reveal a great deal of important information.

Backdrops and props were very popular parts of studio photographs during the late 1800s. How people chose to have themselves or their relatives photographed often reflected their own values and concerns, and sometimes their sense of humor.

The family photograph illustrated here shows some of the problems involved in analyzing a studio picture. It also shows the kind of information that can be found in this type of photograph. The picture shows a child of four or five years of age wearing a skirt and short jacket. The information on the lower margin of the picture tells us that it was taken by a studio photographer named Simcoe, in the town of Marshall, Missouri. The name June Baker is written on the back of the photograph along with the date 1889.

After seeing the name on the back, you might assume that the picture is of a little girl who lived in or near Marshall, Missouri in 1889. June is a common name for a girl and boys usually do not wear skirts! Yet the child has very short hair. So the question arises — is the child a boy or a girl? The date, 1889, might refer to the year the photograph was taken or it might be the year when June was born.

More information must be gathered in order to decide the sex of the child. Talking with older members of the Baker family and examining information in family records reveals that June Baker was a boy. He was born on a farm near Marshall, Missouri, in 1889.

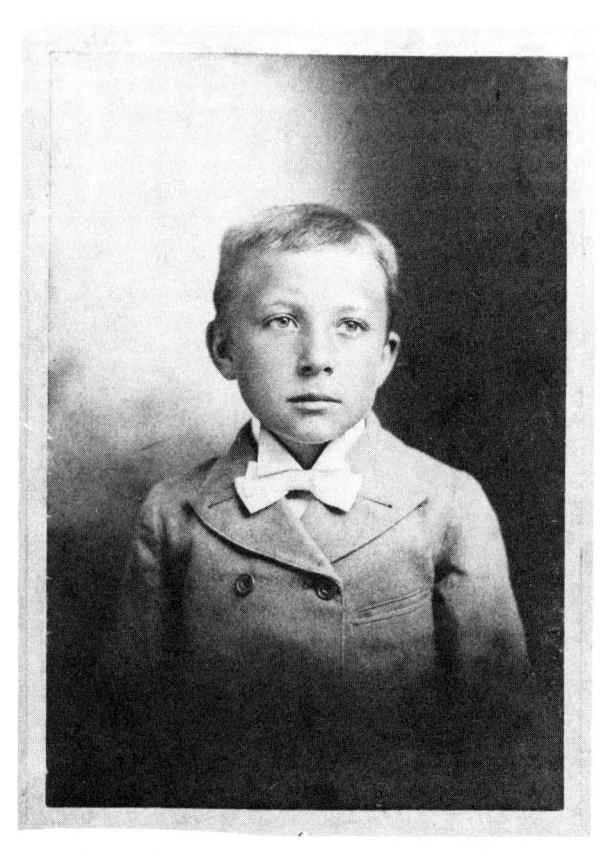

There are several other useful ways to discover more information about a photograph. Compare the picture with others in an album or the family collection. The picture illustrated here is identified on the back as June Baker, seven years of age. The haircut and clothes indicate that the child is a boy. When this photograph is compared with the first one, it appears that they are of the same child.

DIFFERENT TYPES OF HISTORICAL INFORMATION TO BE FOUND IN PHOTOGRAPHS

A closer look at the first photograph can reveal even more information. The fact that the child has his hand on a rail probably means that a long exposure time was necessary to take the picture. Before film was invented in the 1880s photographers had to use wet or dry plates made of glass or metal to take the pictures on. These plates required a much longer exposure time than modern cameras and film.

A baby picture of June Baker dating from 1889 also provides evidence that it was necessary to try to keep the child still. In the lower left-hand corner of the picture, a woman's hand seems to be trying to hold him still. But the child's feet are blurred because he was moving them.

You may find that many old photographs of your own family seem to be very formal. The people in them rarely smile. Sometimes headrests, with braces for the head and neck, were even used to help people sit still for long periods.

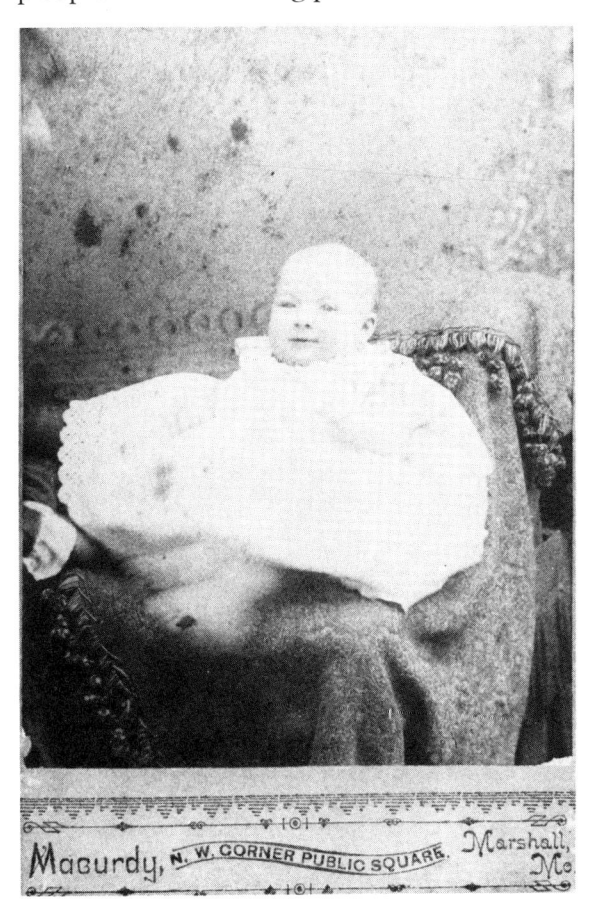

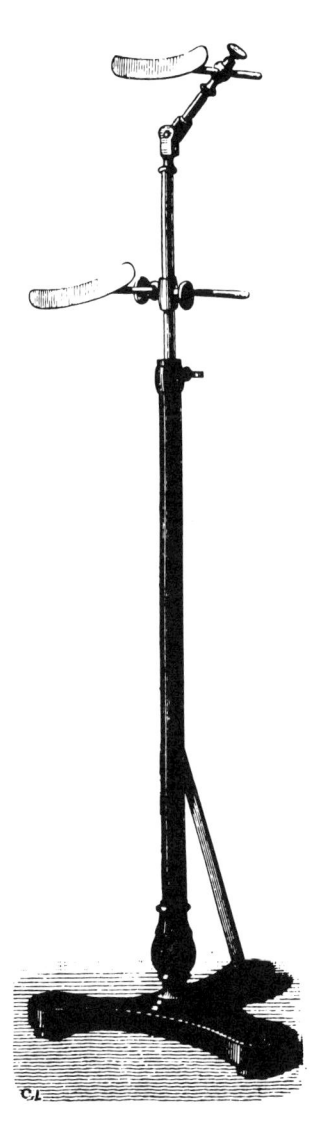

PHOTO DETECTIVE WORK

Some families have photographs that go back many years. Sometimes these pictures are mysteries. You and your family may not know who is in the picture or when and where it was taken. Unfortunately, too many of these pictures will remain a mystery forever unless someone tries to identify them.

Pick five mystery photographs from your family album. Try to discover the following information about the picture:

The subject of each picture.
When it was taken.
Where it was taken.

Write down any other information you can find out about the photograph.

If you don't have any mystery photographs of your own family, you can use the pictures illustrated here to practice photo detective work.

Information may be found on the photographs themselves that will provide important clues. Or it may help to compare these pictures with others in your family's collection. Talk with older members of your family to get answers about the pictures. You may also find it helpful to look at family genealogical records to help identify pictures.

Perhaps all the pictures in your family album are identified. But do they also tell when, where, and why they were taken? This information is also important because it gives the photograph much more meaning. Try to fill in as much missing information as you can on five or more of your favorite mystery photographs.

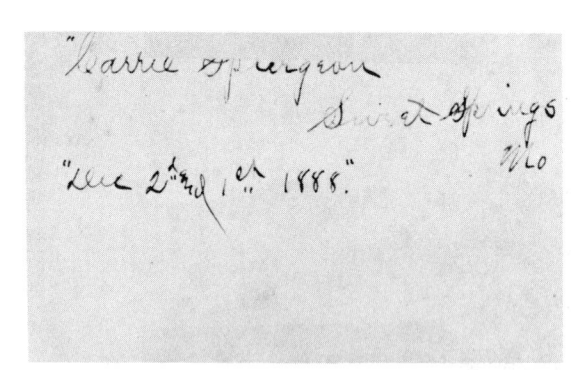

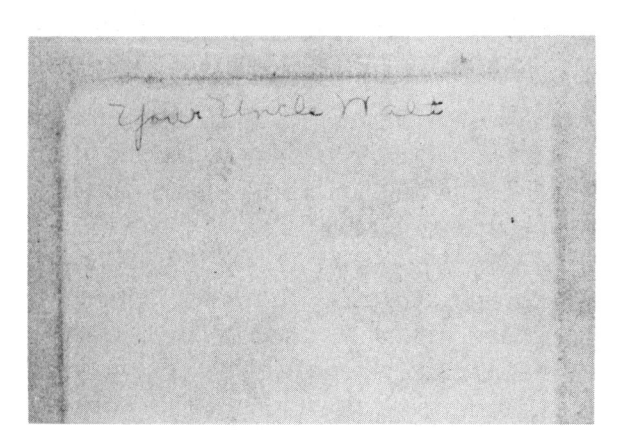

Merry Christmas
to Aunt Susan from
Louise Seymour Gwinn
1897.

Clara L. Martin 1891

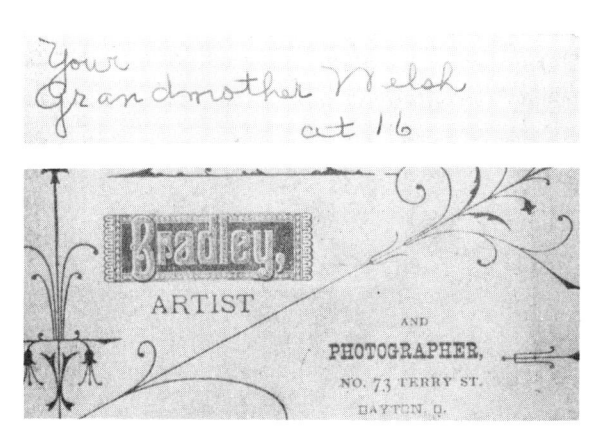

Your
Grandmother Welsh
at 16

Bradley,
ARTIST
AND
PHOTOGRAPHER,
NO. 73 TERRY ST.
DAYTON, O.

East Side Gallery, The Two Johns, Marshall, Mo.

31

Not only can photographs be used as historical documents to identify people, but they can also be used to identify objects. A stickpin found in the Baker family attic would have remained a mystery if it had not been for a studio photograph of John Charles Breckenridge Martin (1864-1947).

If you look closely at the picture you can see a stickpin on the upper left-hand side of Mr. Martin's vest. If you compare it to the stickpin found in the attic, it appears to be the same pin. A part of it has been broken or lost, though.

In this way, objects such as favorite pieces of jewelry or toys that are passed down from generation to generation can be linked to their earlier owners. Sometimes they can even be dated.

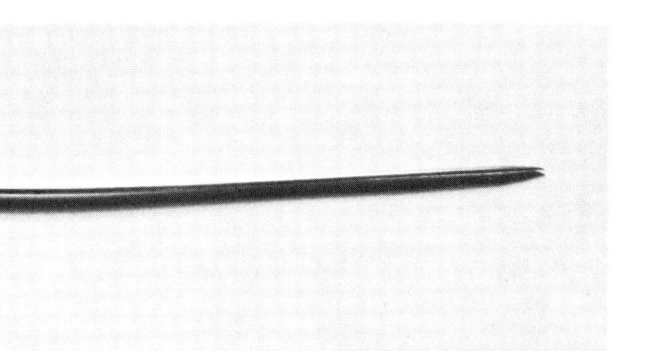

CHILDREN THEN AND NOW

Find a photograph of yourself taken when you were younger. Also try to find one of a grandparent or great-grandparent of the same sex and about the same age.

If you can't find two such photographs in your family album, study the two photographs of a grandmother and her granddaughter illustrated here.

Compare the clothing, hairstyles, and objects included in each photograph. Try to determine when and where each picture was taken. Are they both studio photographs or were they taken by someone in the family? What do the differences in the two photographs tell you about what it was like to be a child in the past compared to when you were younger?

Clara Levenia Martin Baker (1890-1972)

Asterie Patricia Baker (1948-   )

COMPARING HISTORICAL PHOTOGRAPHS FOR MORE INFORMATION

Photographs are often of greatest value to historians when they are compared with other photographs or with different kinds of evidence.

Look at the following three photographs of Pennsylvania Avenue, in Washington, D. C. They were all taken looking toward the Capitol from the steps of the Treasury Building. By closely studying these photographs, you can discover a lot about the history of this section of a famous street.

The earliest photograph dates from 1885. An iron fence encircles the lawn of the Treasury Building in the foreground. Horse-drawn carriages are moving down the street. People are also walking and riding horses on the street. The street itself seems very wide.

Several buildings are located in the left-hand corner of the picture, including the Solaris Hotel. If all you knew was that the photograph was taken in Washington, the name of the hotel might help you identify the street scene. You could look up the hotel in an old city directory to determine its address. If you needed to date the photograph, the Solaris Hotel might also be helpful.

There appear to be some residential buildings on the street, especially the second building from the front, right corner.

(Courtesy The National Archives.)

The second photograph of the same scene dates from 1915. Where the Solaris Hotel used to be now stands a new, larger, building. It appears to be called the Occidental Hotel.

At first glance, the second photograph appears much like the earlier 1885 picture. But careful examination of the photo reveals a very different scene. Many new buildings have been built. The residential building on the right side is gone.

Automobiles have replaced the streetcars. The trees have grown in the second picture. The street appears a bit narrower. Look at the sign painted on the side of the Occidental Hotel. It tells you that a room cost $2.00 a night, and that a Cadillac can be rented for $3.00 an hour. The iron fence is still encircling the Treasury Building lawn, as it does in the third photograph.

(Courtesy The National Archives.)

35

The third photograph dates from 1950. Modern electric streetcars are moving down the street as well as cars. The Occidental Hotel is still there. However, a new building has appeared in the front left corner.

On the opposite side of the street, the scene has also changed. What appear to be government office buildings have taken the place of the older buildings in the two earlier pictures.

When you compare historical photographs such as these three scenes of Pennsylvania Avenue, you may often find that commercial buildings have replaced residences. Sometimes the whole character of a street has changed. You will be able to discover more about the later pictures simply because the earlier photographs will tell you something of the later scene's past.

(Courtesy The National Archives.)

HOW TO FILL OUT A PHOTOGRAPH ANAYLSIS CHART

When so many historical details are provided, it is often easier to interpret the evidence by organizing it on a worksheet like the one illustrated here.

It is important to write down your first impression of the photograph as a brief description. Then you can compare this description with your general conclusions after you have looked at the photograph very closely. This process will help you understand how you made your final interpretations of the picture.

It is also very important to record all the evidence available before you begin to closely analyze the picture and make your interpretations. Be sure to list:

Where the photograph came from.

What condition it is in.

Any written information on the photograph, and so on.

PHOTOGRAPH ANALYSIS CHART

Name of researcher: Date:

Brief description of the photograph (subject and approximate date):

Physical characteristics of the photograph:

Type: Size: Condition:

Source of the photograph:

Identity of the photographer:

Written information on the photograph or in the album:

Important parts and details of the photograph:	Interpretation:

Additional information from other sources:

Conclusions:

Copyright © 1984 by Addison-Wesley Publishing Company

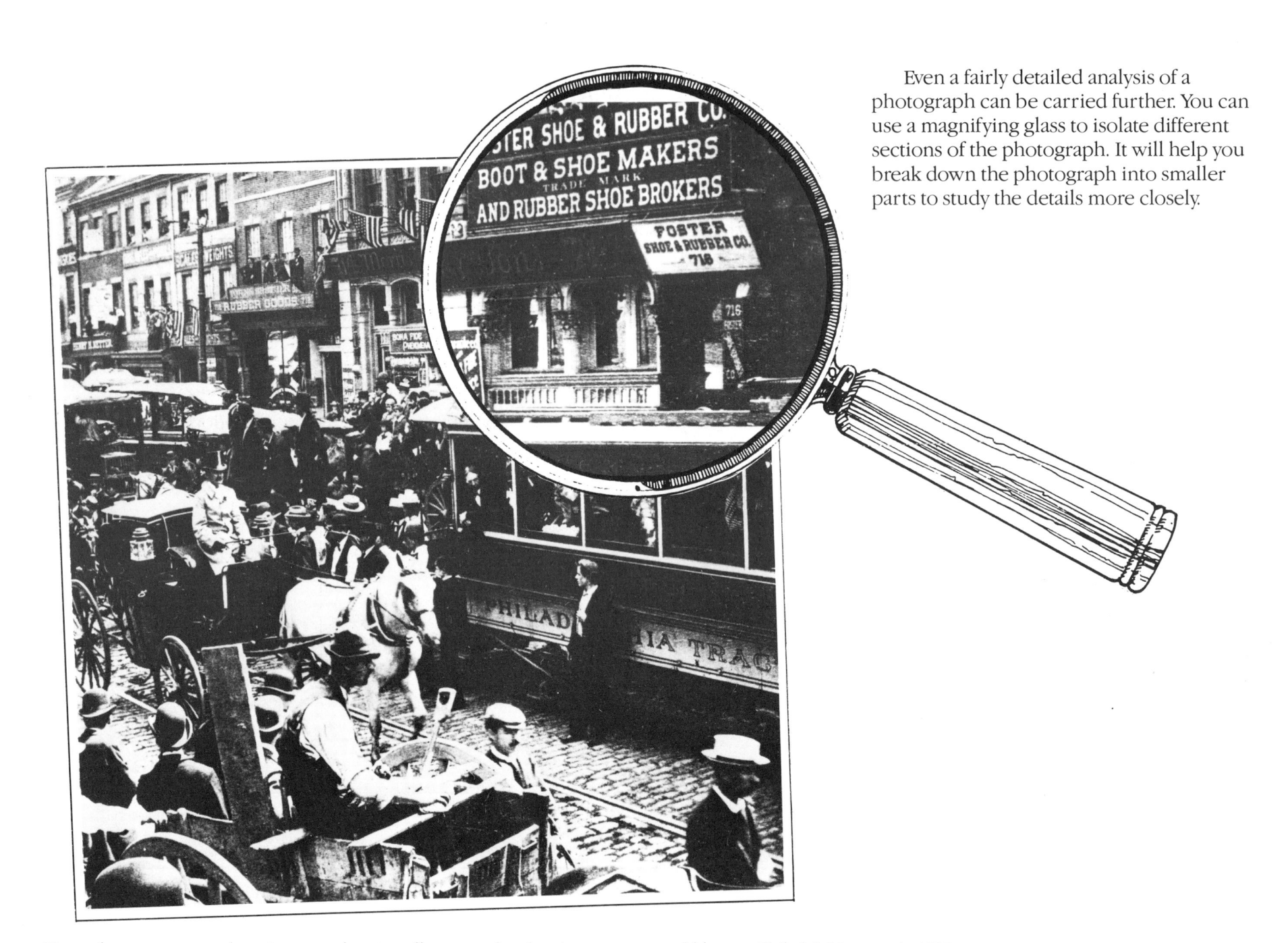

Even a fairly detailed analysis of a photograph can be carried further. You can use a magnifying glass to isolate different sections of the photograph. It will help you break down the photograph into smaller parts to study the details more closely.

Horse-drawn wagons and carriages, an electric trolley car, and pedestrians congest a cobblestone Philadelphia street in 1897. (Courtesy The National Archives.)

ANALYZING PHOTOGRAPHS

The National Archives in Washington, D.C., has over five million photographs. Many of these pictures have been collected as an official record describing things, people, places, and events in the history of the United States.

Look closely at the photographs. Begin your analysis by stating what you see in each picture, without making any assumptions. Then describe the details in each photograph. Break down each photograph in terms of the historical information it provides.

Photocopy or trace the Photograph Analysis Chart included in this book to record all of your observations about each of the four photographs. Fill out a chart for each photograph.

Consider whether or not the picture was posed or if it is a candid shot. Did the photographer arrange the picture or was it taken as an event happened? Think about what the sequence of events might have been just before the photograph was taken.

The captions for these photographs are included on page 53 at the back of *Pursuing The Past*. Look at them after you have completed your analysis of the photographs. Do the captions give away important information about the pictures that you didn't discover in your analysis?

(Courtesy The National Archives.)

39

(Courtesy The National Archives.)

(Courtesy The National Archives.)

(Courtesy The National Archives.)

(Photographs courtesy the National Air and Space Museum.)

After looking closely at the different parts of a photograph, you may decide that it is necessary to search for more information in outside sources. Family records may identify a person. Information about the photographer may tell you when and why the picture was taken. It may also tell you something about the photographer's point of view. Or you may need to check city maps and street directories to identify a street scene. Newspapers and general history books may help to put a particular event within the correct historical context and complete the picture for you.

43

RECONSTRUCTING COMMUNITY HISTORY

Collections of photographs or old postcards depicting the history of a community are often available for use at your local historical society. Libraries, municipal record offices, as well as published histories of your community, may also have old photographs.

Important evidence of a community's past may also be found in private collections of photographs. Many of these pictures were probably kept as records of people, not places. Yet buildings and street scenes may appear in the background.

Try to find photographs that will help you reconstruct the history of your community. Focus on a particular street, the town square, or a park. Or you may reconstruct the history of a building such as a school, grocery store, or church.

If actual photographs are not available to you, make photocopies of those you can find in books or from museums. Mount these pictures in chronological order. Analyze each of them on a Photograph Analysis Chart. Then write a short paragraph under each photograph that describes the date of the picture and the important facts about it.

Be sure to compare the photographs to each other. Comment on changes in the buildings, streets, and means of transportation. Also note what has remained unchanged in the chronological sequence you have created.

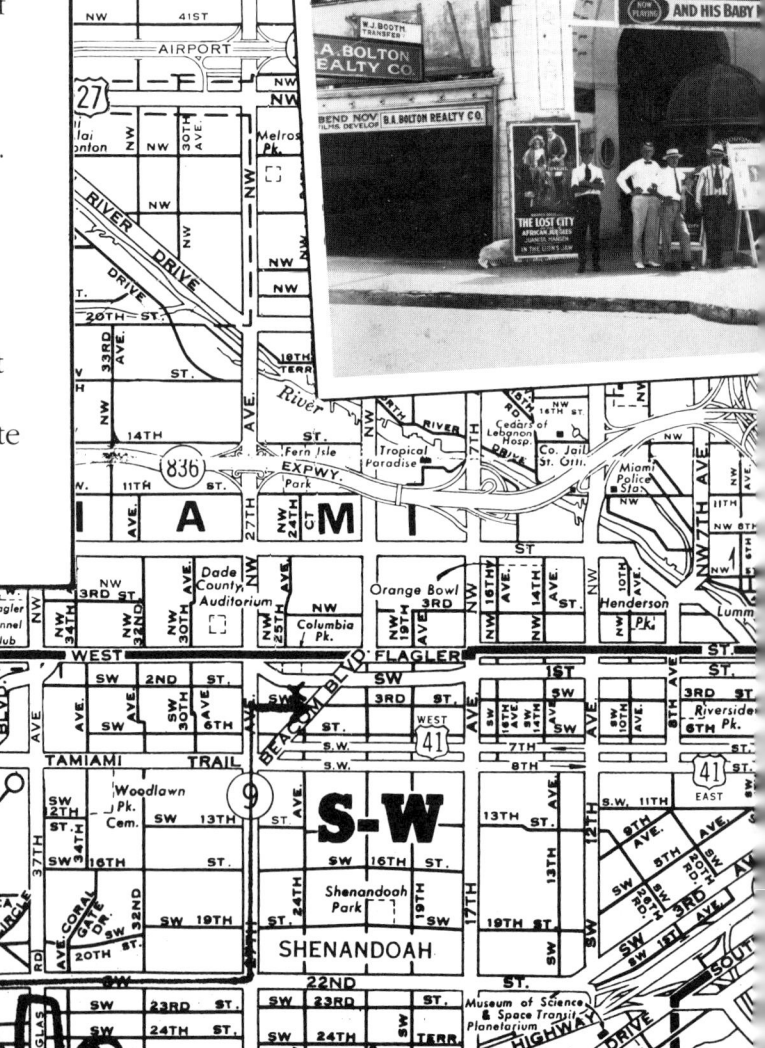

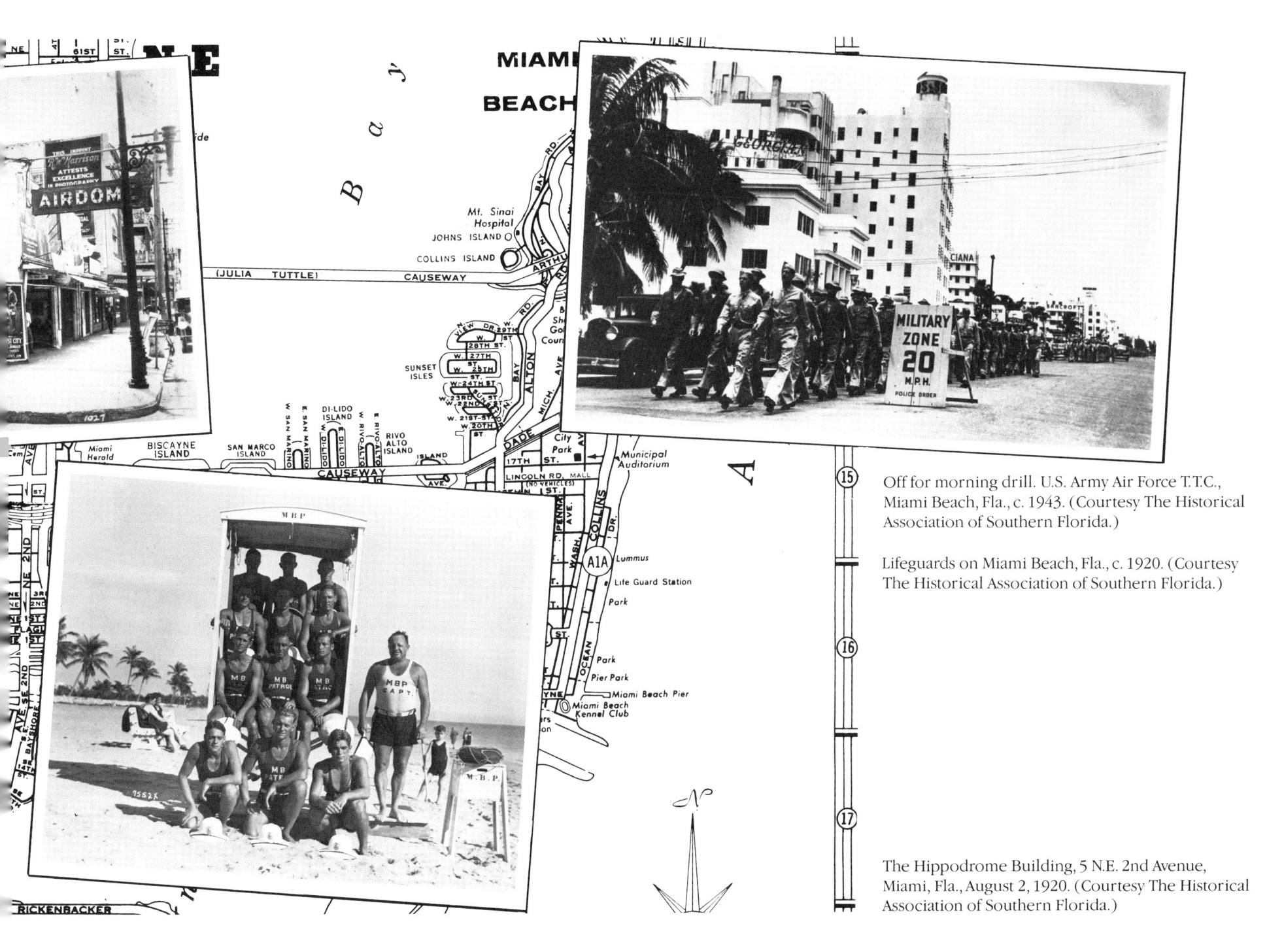

Off for morning drill. U.S. Army Air Force T.T.C., Miami Beach, Fla., c. 1943. (Courtesy The Historical Association of Southern Florida.)

Lifeguards on Miami Beach, Fla., c. 1920. (Courtesy The Historical Association of Southern Florida.)

The Hippodrome Building, 5 N.E. 2nd Avenue, Miami, Fla., August 2, 1920. (Courtesy The Historical Association of Southern Florida.)

45

FAKED AND ALTERED PHOTOGRAPHS

Careful critical judgment must be used in analyzing a photograph. Often people assume that as a reflection of real life a photograph is an accurate historical document. Yet photographs can easily be faked or altered in such a way as to show only certain types of information.

An example of altering historical photographs was described to the authors by a well-known publisher of books on railroad history. Often these books include pictures of huge steam engines with billows of smoke pouring from their smokestacks. The publisher described how a collection of pictures of smokestacks with smoke pouring out of them was taken in Pittsburgh, Pennsylvania. The smoke from these photographs was then imposed onto a photograph of a steam engine in operation. While the effect may have been very dramatic, it had little to do with historical reality!

Any photograph involves a choice made by the photographer. When photographers frame their pictures they limit what the viewer sees. The meaning of the photograph depends upon how it is framed.

Photographs themselves can be altered by cropping them so that certain parts of the picture are removed. In this way the subject matter, meaning, and historical value of the photograph can be changed completely.

It is often very difficult to tell if a photograph has been faked or altered. However, when you use or interpret a photograph as a historical document, you should keep this possibility in mind.

(Courtesy The National Archives.)

A U. S. O. Christmas Event in Europe in 1944, or, recent masquerade party.

STAGING A PHOTOGRAPH

Perhaps one of the best ways to learn about faked or altered photographs is to stage your own photograph. It might be:

> An illustration for an advertisement.
>
> For a newspaper story.
>
> For a magazine article.
>
> A portrait of someone.
>
> A record of an event.

Consider what to use as a backdrop or background for the photograph you are going to create. Decide how many people will be in the picture. How will they be dressed? What will they be doing? How will these people relate to one another? Also pick what objects will be included in the picture and whether or not the people will be handling any of these props.

Now you can see why it is important to carefully analyze a photograph and to collect as much evidence about it from outside sources as possible. In this way, you will be doing the best job you possibly can in solving the historical mysteries that photographs present.

Remember, from the moment a photograph is taken, it becomes an historical document. Be sure to identify and preserve the photographs you take yourself throughout your life.

49

A carte de visite from the 1880s.

HOW TO HANDLE PHOTOGRAPHS AS HISTORICAL DOCUMENTS

If you are taking photographs out of an album, be sure to make a list of where they were placed so that the sequence won't be destroyed.

Always handle photographs and negatives at the edges. Do not touch the surface of the film or emulsion of a negative.

Do not bend photographs or carry or store them so that they can be bent.

Always wash your hands before handling negatives because oil from your fingers can permanently mark the film. Negatives should be dusted with a soft brush and then stored in envelopes where dust can't collect on them. Be sure to label the envelopes.

If you happen to find any old rolls of developed film, be sure to unroll them very carefully because they may be brittle. Every time film is wound and unwound, the emulsion can be scratched. Cut the film into strips so that it can also be stored in envelopes.

PHOTOCOPYING PHOTOGRAPHS

Whenever you want to make a copy of a photograph and you can't get a photographic copy made, make a photocopy of it instead. Often it is a good idea to make photocopies of old photographs to mail to relatives or to carry around with you, so that the real photograph isn't handled too much and possibly damaged.

Arrange the photographs face down on the screen of the photocopying machine. The copies may come out clearer if you push the "extra dark" button or ask the machine operator to make extra dark copies.

TYPES OF PHOTOGRAPHS AND PHOTOGRAPHIC PROCESSES

The following descriptions of photographic processes are included to help you identify and date old photographs.

DAGUERREOTYPE

The first successful photographic process and picture was the daguerreotype. An image was formed on a copper plate coated with polished silver by using vapors from heated mercury. The process was invented in the late 1830s by the Frenchman Louis Daguerre (1789-1851).

Only one daguerreotype photograph could be made from a plate. The positive image on it was always reversed from what it was in real life.

Daguerreotypes could be purchased for about two dollars in the 1840s. They usually came in standard sizes and were often matted and framed in brass.

Since daguerreotypes required long exposures, their subjects had to be formally and stiffly posed. People in them rarely smiled. Headrests and props were often used to help people hold still.

WET-PLATE PROCESS

In the wet-plate or collodion process, invented by the English sculptor Frederick Archer in 1851, any number of positive prints could be made from a glass plate negative.

Wet-plate negatives could not be enlarged. Therefore, the camera and the wet-plate had to be as large as the desired print. Since strong artifical light hadn't been developed, wet-plate photographs could not be taken inside or at night.

Extremely inexpensive photographs known as ambrotypes could be produced by the wet-plate process. They were very popular in the United States throughout the 1850s. Like daguerreotypes, they came in standard sizes and were often matted, then framed in elaborate gilded-brass frames that came in protective cases.

TINTYPE

Introduced in 1852, tintype positive images were made directly on thin tin plates. The plates were enameled with a sensitized coating.

Tintypes were easy and cheap to make. They were also stronger than glass plates and could easily be exchanged through the mail. During the late 1800s, hundreds of thousands of Americans had tintype portraits made in studios.

CARTE DE VISITE

This inexpensive process was patented in 1854 by the Frenchman André Adolphe-Eugene Disdéri. The name carte de visite is the name given both to his special camera and to the photographs themselves. Carte de visite cameras had four or more lenses. They took multiple images on a single wet-plate negative.

The large positive print was cut into individual photographs that usually measured 3 1/2 inches by 2 1/8 inches. They were attached to cards the size of calling cards or visiting cards. Since these inexpensive portraits were often left by visitors in place of printed calling cards, they became known as cartes de visite (French for "calling card").

STEREOSCOPIC PHOTOGRAPHS

By the 1840s, stereoscopic photographs were being taken, which could be viewed through stereoscopes to produce a three-dimensional effect.

Cameras with special systems of lenses took two slightly different pictures of the same object at once. Each lens was 2 1/2 inches from the other so that the two different pictures recorded were exactly what would be seen by your eyes. When placed in a stereoscope, the two images were combined to produce a three-dimensional view.

During the second half of the nineteenth century, throughout Europe and the United States, photographers took stereoscopic views of many famous places and events. Niagara Falls, World's Fairs, and the Western frontier as well as funny and sentimental scenes were viewed by thousands of Americans who collected stereoscopic cards.

DRY-PLATE PROCESS

The dry-plate process was discovered in 1871 by the English physician, Dr. Richard L. Maddox. It made it possible for photographers to carry only a camera and a few loaded dry-plate holders. The plates could be exposed wherever the picture was taken and then developed back in the photographer's darkroom.

Since the required exposure time had also been reduced, photographers were able to shoot less formal poses. The dry-plate method made it much easier to take photographs anywhere. Both amateur and professional photographers could buy dry plates already manufactured. They either developed them themselves or sent the exposed plates to a developing company to make the prints for them.

FLEXIBLE ROLL-FILM CAMERAS

Invented in the early 1880s by George Eastman, flexible roll film made the process of taking pictures even easier. At first a roll of paper treated with gelatin was used. Rolls of transparent plastic were soon developed which gave birth to modern photographic film. Rolls of film were held in position by roll holders which could be fitted onto any standard-plate camera.

Eastman still searched for an even easier method of photography. In 1888, he invented a box camera (6" x 3 1/2" x 4") that was pre-loaded with flexible roll film of 100 frames. Eastman named the camera Kodak.

When you finished taking 100 exposures the camera, which was still loaded with film, was mailed to Eastman's factory. For $10.00 you received the camera back, loaded with an unexposed roll of film. The negatives and circular prints mounted on cards were also returned within 10 days.

Stereoscope card of the Paris Exposition, 1857.

Shorter exposure times and faster shutters made possible the development of the Kodak camera and the famous Brownie in 1900. These cameras introduced millions of children, women and men throughout the world to the fun of taking their own candid snapshot photographs.

POLAROID CAMERA

Invented in 1947 by Edwin Land, the Polaroid camera processed its own film right in the camera. By 1963, the Polaroid Land camera was able to produce color photographs.

Eastman Kodak Co.'s BROWNIE CAMERAS $1.00

Make pictures 2¼ x 2¼ inches. Load In Daylight with our six exposure film cartridges and are so simple they can be easily **Operated by Any School Boy or Girl.** Fitted with fine Meniscus lenses and our improved rotary shutters for snap shots or time exposures. Strongly made, covered with imitation leather, have nickeled fittings and produce the best results.

Brownie Camera, for 2¼ x 2¼ pictures, - - $1.00
Transparent-Film Cartridge, 6 exposures, 2¼ x 2¼, - .15
Brownie Developing and Printing Outfit, - - .75

Ask your dealer or write us for a Brownie Camera Club Constitution. $500.00 in Kodak prizes to the members.

EASTMAN KODAK CO.,
Rochester, N. Y.

An early advertisement for Brownie cameras.

$2.10 TO $4.75 ACCORDING TO SIZE.

A developing, finishing, and material outfit for either plate cameras or film cameras advertised in the Sears, Roebuck and Company catalog in 1908.

"'Okies' car driving through town," by Harmon, Amarillo, Texas, July 1941. (Courtesy The National Archives.)

"Eighteen miles from Stanton. 'Board and lodging' en route for Stanton," by A. J. Buck, Fort Stanton, New Mexico, date unknown. (Courtesy The National Archives.)

"One room school at Versylvania in a converted two room dwelling. Of 15 pupils, six were absent the day the picture was taken," by Irving Rusinow, Taos, New Mexico, December 1941. (Courtesy The National Archives.)

"A family watches a debate between John F. Kennedy and Richard Nixon during the presidential election. September 26, 1960," photographer unknown, United Press International. (Courtesy The National Archives.)

Mrs. W. J. Sprow
1211 Wayne St
Sandusky Ohio

FAMILY HISTORY

Chapter 3: FAMILY HISTORY

Family history and genealogy are among the most popular types of historical research, and almost certainly the oldest. At the beginning of the Bible in the Book of Genesis, for example, one of the oldest and probably the best known of all family histories can be found:

> When Adam had lived a hundred and thirty years, he became the father of a son in his own likeness, after his image, and named him Seth…When Seth had lived a hundred and five years, he became the father of Enosh…When Enosh had lived ninety years, he became the father of Kenan…

The genealogy of the family of Adam continues for eleven generations down through the sons of Noah.

Adam
Seth
Enosh
Kenan
Mahalalel
Jared
Enoch
Methuselah
Lamech
Noah
Ham

Many types of historical records are used in tracing family histories. Among the most important are census records. Usually, a census is an official count of people along with information such as their sex and age.

The oldest European census dates from A.D. 1085. It was commissioned by William the Conqueror (1027?-1087), the first Norman king of England. Known as the *Domesday Book*, this census recorded every field, domestic animal, and human being in England. Regular censuses were begun in the United States in 1790 and in England in 1801.

Other records that will help you discover your family history include tax records, land records, wills, and birth, death, and marriage certificates. Births, marriages, and deaths are often listed in the front or middle of family Bibles. Diaries, old letters, newspapers, report cards, and even general history books are also good sources.

The discovery of your family's past can be very exciting. Too often people have traced their genealogies hoping to discover that they are related to some famous person. You would be proud to find that you are related to the English queen, Victoria; or to the abolitionist, Frederick Douglass; or to the American Indian, Sitting Bull. However, it can be just as fun to find out why your great-great-grandfather fled Germany in the 1840s and what he did when he arrived in Ohio as an immigrant.

By tracking down this type of information, you are not simply making a collection of names and dates. You are re-creating the lives of your ancestors. Not only can family history bring you closer to your relatives but it can also make you feel more a part of your family and its history.

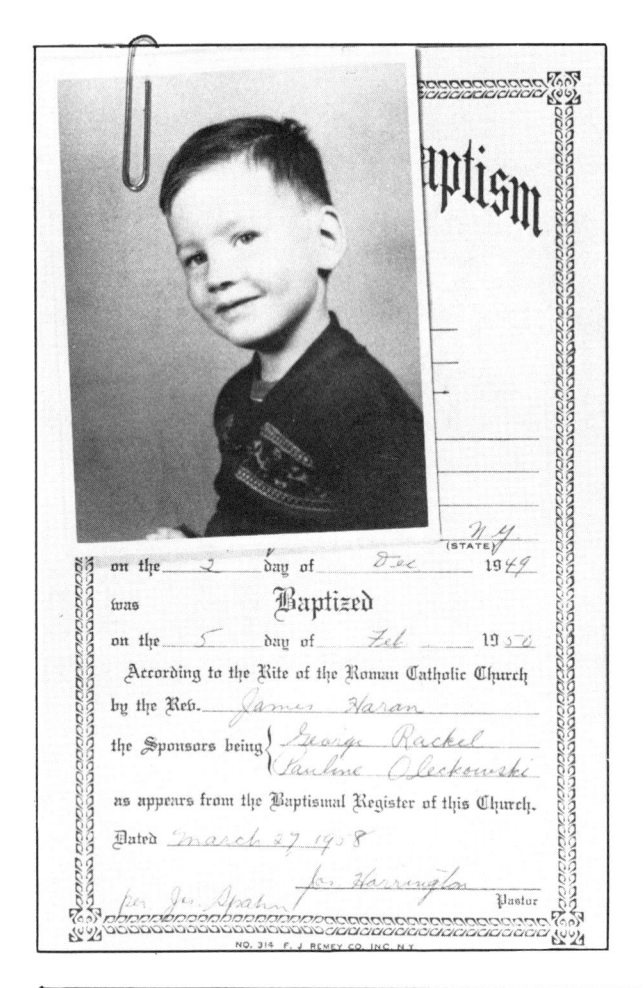

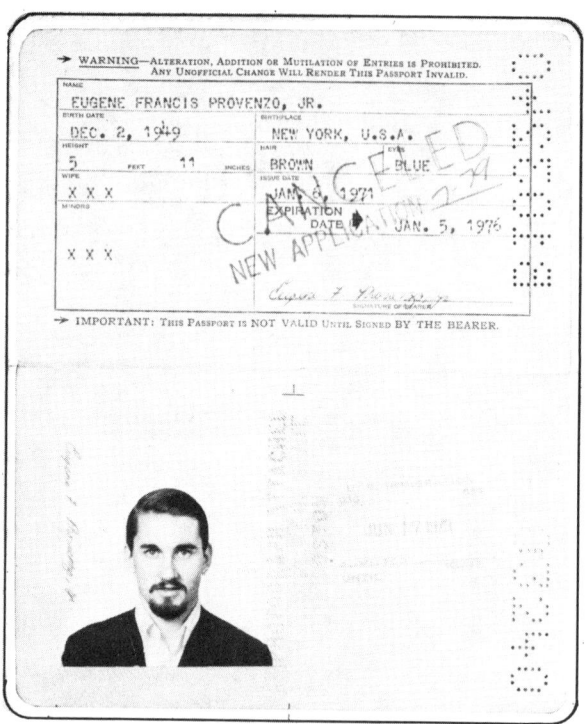

COLLECT YOUR OWN HISTORY

One of the best ways to begin to discover your family history is to start with yourself. You can probably find lots of photographs of yourself around the house. Some of them will remind you of important events in your own life.

Ask your parents to help you locate any documents about you, such as birth certificates, baptismal certificates, report cards, and award certificates. These documents might also help you reconstruct important events in your life. Try to match up photographs with documents to see what you looked like when these events happened.

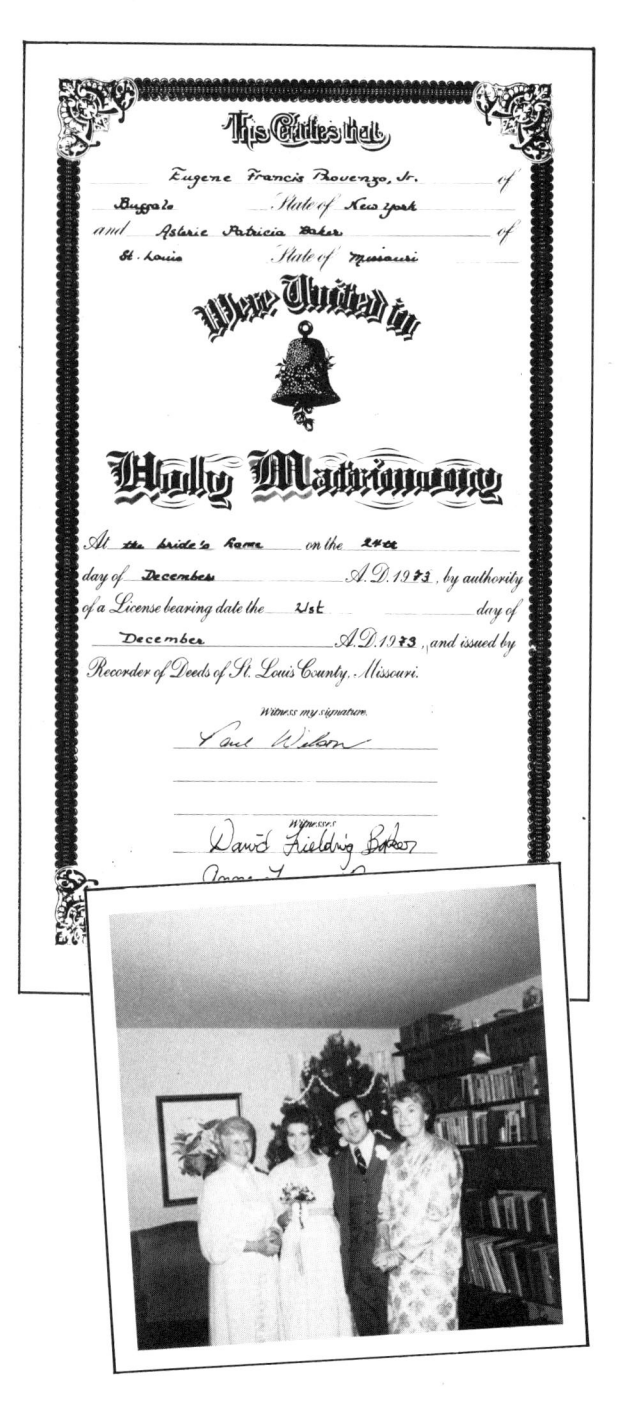

61

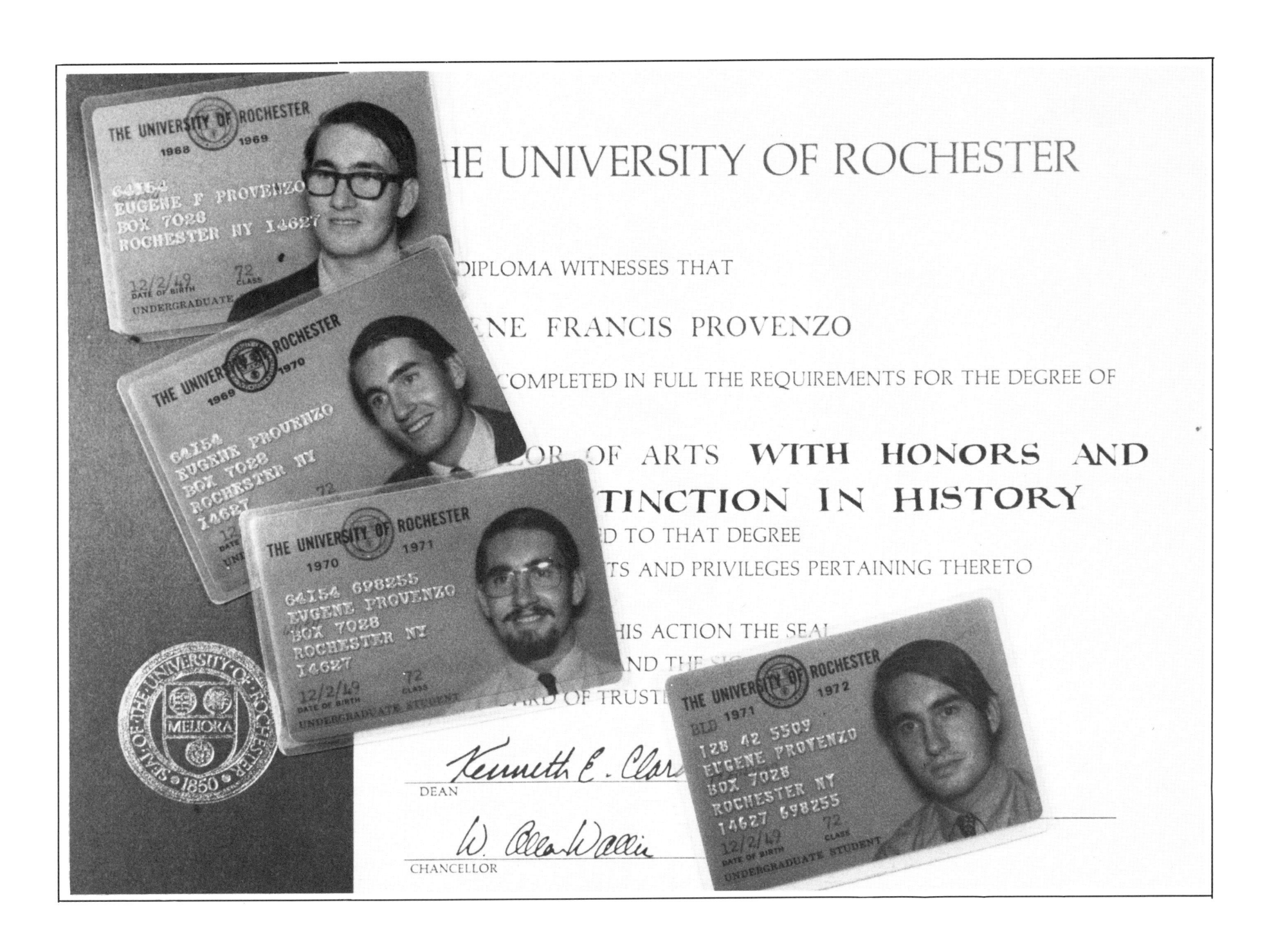

FILLING OUT A FAMILY DATA SHEET

It should be easy to identify the relationship of different members of your family. You can also collect their vital statistics — the dates and places of their births, marriages, and so on.

Copy, by placing a piece of tracing paper over the page, or by photocopying, the Individual Data Sheet provided in this book. Do not write on the chart in the book because you or someone else may want to use it more than once.

Fill out the data sheet for your own immediate family. Be sure to list the sources of your information, such as interviews with family members, family Bibles, birth certificates, and so on, in the spaces provided.

When filling in your chart, be sure to use a pencil since it is easier to erase. Always write in a person's full, original name. Write in the day, month, and year for all dates. It is better to write out the name of the month, rather than using a numeral. Always be sure to write the complete year, not just the last two numerals.

The "No.____" before the person's legal name is where you fill in what number the person is on your ancestor chart. This will be explained later, when you fill out your ancestor chart.

INDIVIDUAL DATA SHEET

SOURCES OF INFORMATION

No._____ Legal name _____
(male or female)   first   middle   last

_____

Nicknames or name changes _____

_____

Date of birth _____ Place of birth _____

_____

No._____ Father's name _____
                         first   middle   last

_____

Date of birth _____ Place of birth _____

_____

Date of marriage _____ Place of marriage _____ Marriage ended _____

Date of death _____ Place of death _____ Buried at _____

Other wives (if any)
_____

No._____ Mother's name _____
                         first   middle   last (maiden)

Date of birth _____ Place of birth _____

Date of marriage _____ Place of marriage _____ Marriage ended _____

Date of death _____ Place of death _____ Buried at _____

Other husbands (if any)
_____

Other children (brothers and sisters)

male or female	Name	Date of birth	Where	Married to	When	Date of death	Where

Copyright © 1984 by Addison-Wesley Publishing Company

63

TURNING DATA INTO FAMILY HISTORY

To turn the data you have collected and recorded into family history, try to fill in some of the gaps in your own vital statistics. Answer the following questions from your own memory and by talking with the other members of your family:

What was the day like when you were born?

When did you first walk?

When did you first talk?

What were your first words?

When were your brothers and sisters born? Do you remember their births?

What was the first house like that you remember living in?

Has your family ever moved? What do you remember about these moves?

What was your first school like?

What is your earliest memory?

Where did you go on the first trip you remember?

What is the first television program you remember watching?

What is the first major national event you remember? Why do you remember it?

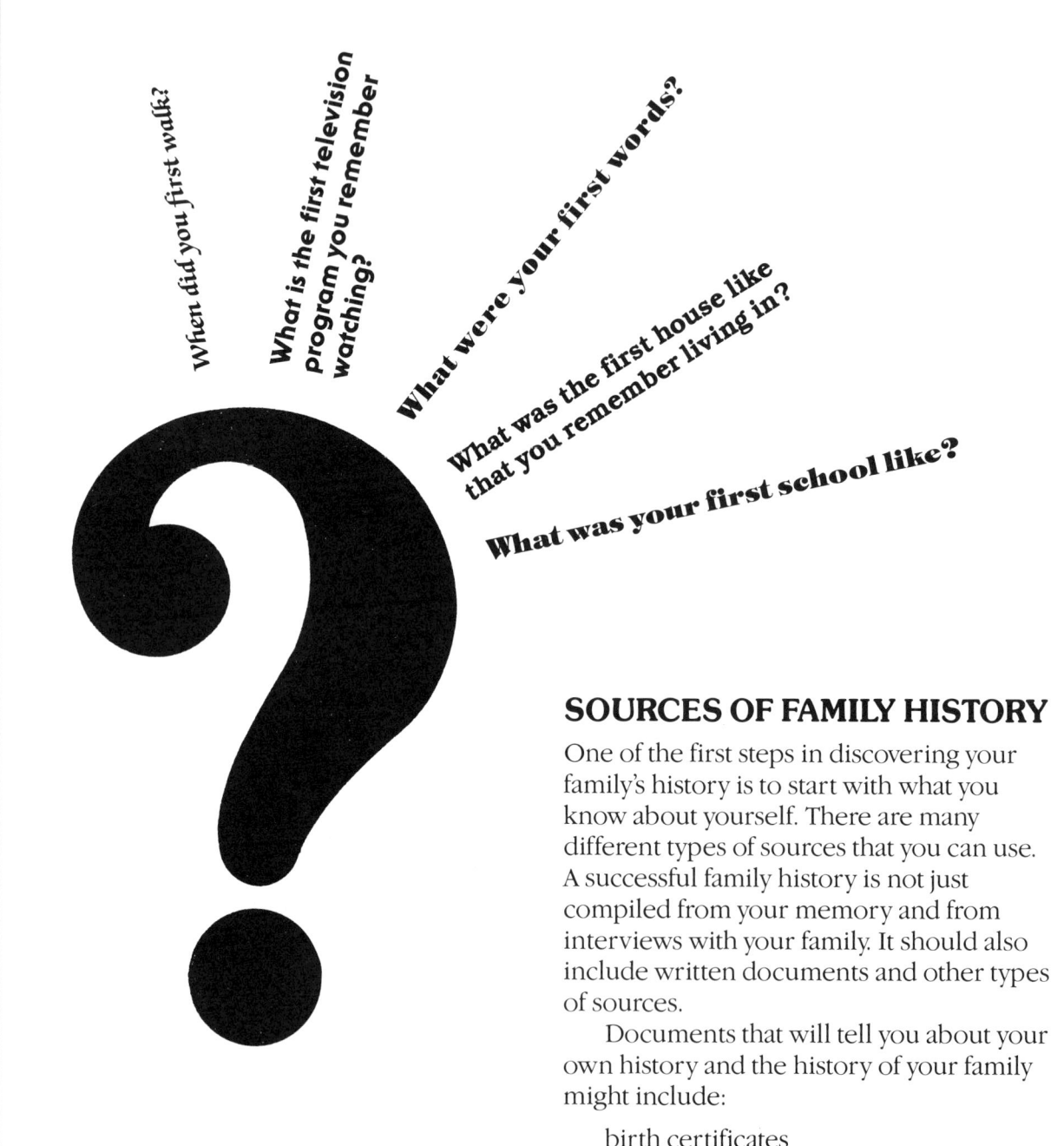

When did you first walk?

What is the first television program you remember watching?

What were your first words?

What was the first house like that you remember living in?

What was your first school like?

SOURCES OF FAMILY HISTORY

One of the first steps in discovering your family's history is to start with what you know about yourself. There are many different types of sources that you can use. A successful family history is not just compiled from your memory and from interviews with your family. It should also include written documents and other types of sources.

Documents that will tell you about your own history and the history of your family might include:

> birth certificates

family Bibles

old photograph albums

trophies

old letters

newspaper clippings

baby books

report cards

diaries

For example, an old letter found in a box of family photographs and letters might confirm that one of your relatives was adopted. If you read the letter carefully, you may discover exactly how they became a member of your family. They may actually have been left on a front doorstep! Whenever you find an old letter, always keep it with its original envelope. The postmark on the envelope might help date the letter.

As a detective hot on the trail of your family's history you will often have to be skeptical about many of the facts you uncover. For example, suppose you discover that all of the data about births and deaths included in your family Bible are written in the same handwriting and in the same color of ink. This probably means that the information was copied down by one person from another source or even from memory. Suppose you discover that many of the dates recorded in the Bible are before the date when the Bible was printed. This would indicate that the earlier dates were copied from another source.

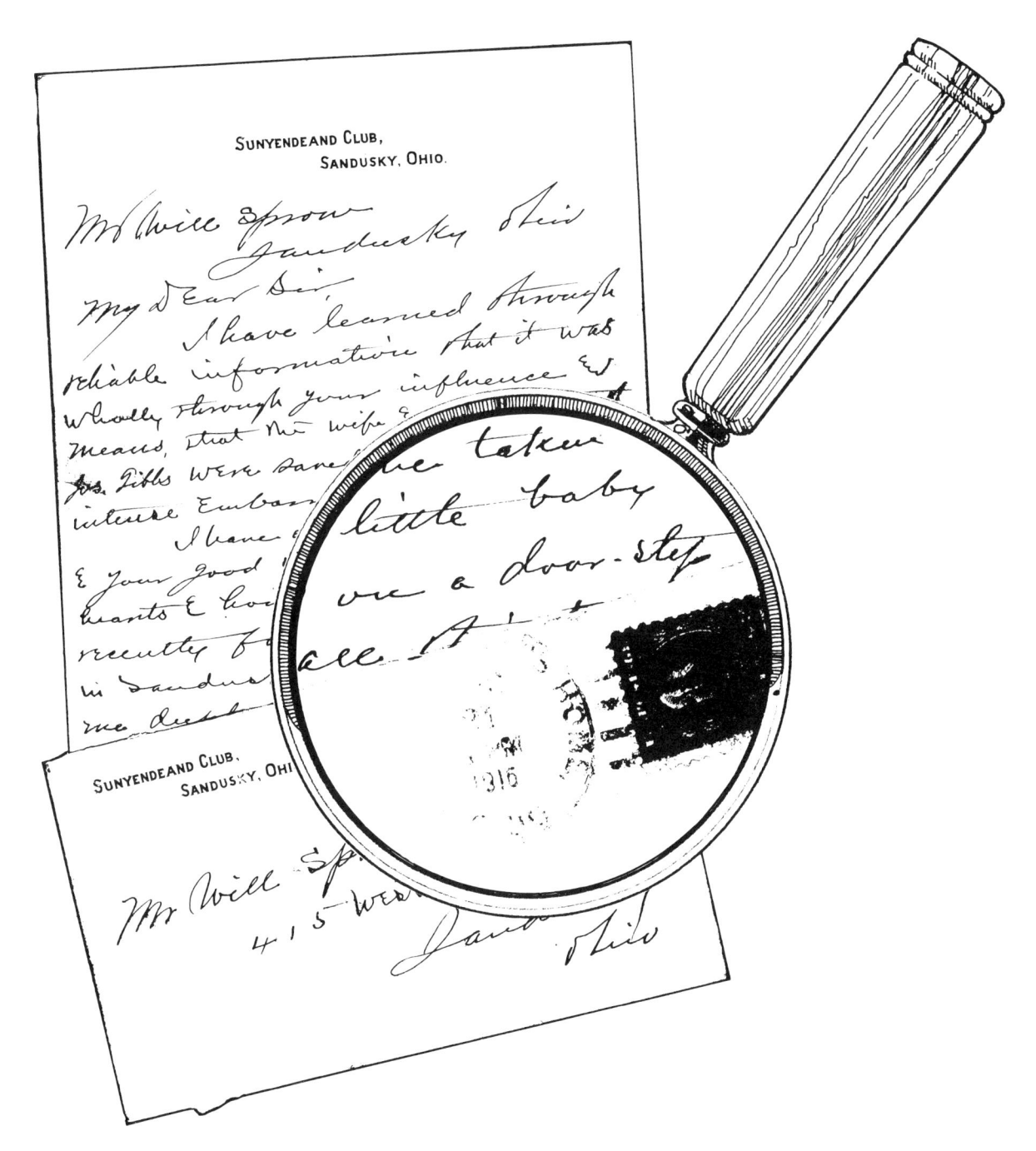

65

A TIMELINE OF YOUR OWN LIFE

An easy way to organize the information that you have discovered about your own life is to put it onto a timeline. Draw a straight line across several pieces of paper that are pasted together. Start the timeline with the date of your birth. Mark off equal spaces on the line for each year that you have lived.

Ask relatives or family friends what important events they can remember about your life when you were younger. Do they remember you having any diseases or accidents? What was your first birthday party like? When and where did you first go to school? Has your family ever moved? Think about your favorite teachers and classmates. When did you meet them? Have you won any awards or events?

Be very careful about recording dates on the timeline so that they are in correct chronological order. Carefully enter the information you have discovered about yourself on your timeline. You may want to expand the timeline and illustrate it with photographs or drawings.

By compiling a timeline about yourself and filling in more than just the vital statistics, you have taken a big step in putting together your own family history.

1948	1949	1950	1951
Born: March 2, 1948. With my mother, grandmother, and great-grandmother in Virginia	With my parents and my first birthday cake — blowing out the candle.	Visiting my grandparents on their farm in Missouri. They had an attic, cows and kittens	Talking with my cousin Pam. We moved to Pittsburg, Kansas

WRITING YOUR AUTOBIOGRAPHY

Your timeline can provide the basis for writing your autobiography. Use the information that you have collected for your timeline as an outline for writing an essay about yourself.

Fill in the details about your first day at school. Write about how you met your first good friend and the types of things you did together. Include information about some of your favorite things: jokes, foods, games, books, television programs, and movies.

Your autobiography should become part of the family history that you are assembling. Keep it safe, along with the other documents and information you have collected. It can be passed on to future generations.

My brother, Davy, was born this year. I liked to play with him and Jill, our next-door neighbor	My best friend Dougie and his sister, Jody. All the neighborhood kids in our costumes for the "Nutcracker Suite"	My first-grade school picture. I went to Horace Mann Elementary School.	With my brother on our trip to Virginia to see our great-grandmother.
1952	1953	1954	1955

It is the family historian's job to discover as many facts as possible about a family, even those hidden in legend. Not everyone can be related to George Washington! But you do have 1024 great-great-great-great-great-great-great-great-grandparents.

67

TRACKING DOWN FAMILY STORIES

Even a recent relative can be a fascinating source of history. Nicholas Provenzo, grandfather of one of the authors, came from Cefalu, Sicily, sometime around 1900. Family stories tell about him getting a start as a newsboy in Buffalo, New York, and eventually becoming a successful businessman. Much of the information about Nicholas Provenzo has become confused over the years.

He died just weeks before his second child, Eugene, was born. Some stories tell that he died of a heart attack when he was thirty-seven years old. Others say that he died when he was thirty-four from severe stomach problems. By going through old family documents such as newspaper clippings and photographs, we can begin to pick up some clues as to what actually happened.

A newspaper clipping included in the family album describes Nick Provenzo's death. It also gives a great deal of information about his life. Let's take a closer look at his newspaper obituary:

Location of hotel owned by Nicholas Provenzo — 128 Seneca Street, Buffalo, New York.

He was a former newsboy and saloon keeper.

A description of his death.

He ran a newsstand at Main and Chippewa Streets in Buffalo for twelve years. Eight years before his death he bought a saloon on Washington Street with the savings from his paper sales.

We learn something about his personality and popularity.

About three years before his death he bought a saloon, bowling alley, and hotel. It was here that he died.

He lived in an apartment at the hotel.

He had been ill the day before his death.

Since Nick Provenzo died at the age of thirty-four, and we learned that he bought the saloon about eight years earlier, we can conclude that he must have been about twenty-six years old when he bought it. If he ran a newsstand for twelve years prior to buying the saloon, then he must have set up the newsstand when he was about fourteen years old!

"NICK PROVENZO" DIES SUDDENLY IN HIS HOTEL

Well Known Figure Collapses and Expires Before Medical Aid Arrives—Got His Start as Newsboy.

"Nick" Provenzo is dead.

His body was found this morning by Patrolman William Marks of the Franklin street station on the second floor of a hotel at No. 128 Seneca street, of which the dead man was proprietor. Natural causes are believed to have caused the death of the former newsboy and saloonkeeper.

Marks was standing in front of the Broezel hotel when he discerned the form of Provenzo standing close to the front window of the hotel across the street. Suddenly Provenzo fell and the patrolman ran to the room. Provenzo was lying on the floor. A doctor was called but pronounced him dead.

"Nick" Provenzo was known to nearly every man about town. He secured his start as a newsboy. For twelve years he had a stand at Main and Chippewa streets. About eight years ago, from the savings of his paper sales, he bought a saloon in Washington street

near Huron street. In those days the saloon was known as one of the liveliest in town and Nick's smiling face became known to every man who ever frequented the place.

When the cabaret business waned about three years ago Provenzo bought a saloon, bowling alley and hotel at the Seneca street address. He has been conducting the place since, living in one of the apartments.

Provenzo suffered from cramps yesterday and was in bed. He arose this morning, apparently in good condition, and was on his way to open the bar when he collapsed and died.

Provenzo was 34 years old.

NICK PROVENZO DROPS DEAD IN HIS HOTEL

Nicholas Provenzo, former secretary of the Newsboys' association, and at one time one of the best known carriers of the EVENING NEWS in the business district of the city, died suddenly this morning in his hotel at 128 Seneca street. He had been in the hotel business for several years. Physicians who were summoned said death was due to heart disease.

Provenzo was 37 years old. He is survived by his widow and one child.

My Jesus have mercy on the soul of

Nicholas Provenzo

DIED AUGUST 21, 1920

PRAYER

O gentlest Heart of Jesus, ever present in the Blessed Sacrament, ever consumed with burning love for the poor captive souls in Purgatory have mercy on the soul of Thy departed servant. Be not severe in thy judgment but let some drops of Thy Precious Blood fall upon the devouring flames, and do Thou O Merciful Saviour, send Thy angels to conduct Thy departed servant to a place of refreshment, light and peace. Amen.

May the souls of all the faithful departed through the mercy of God, rest in peace. Amen.

Eternal rest grant unto them, O Lord! And let perpetual light shine upon them. Sacred Heart of Jesus have mercy on them Immaculate Heart of Mary, pray for them. St. Joseph, friend of the Sacred Heart, pray for them.

(100 days for each aspiration)

SOLACE ART CO., P. O. BOX 7, STATION E BROOKLYN, N.Y.

Another newspaper clipping explains some of the family's confusion about Nick Provenzo. This clipping describes Nicholas Provenzo as the former secretary of the newsboys' association and one of the best-known carriers of the *Buffalo Evening News*. It also relates that his death was caused by a heart attack when he was thirty-seven years old.

These two newspaper clippings show that even the printed word cannot always be trusted when you are compiling a family history or genealogy. Double-checking your facts is always important. By searching for Nick Provenzo's official death certificate or naturalization papers, or by contacting an older relative, it should be possible to determine which information is correct.

Other documents provide more information about Nick Provenzo's life. Included in a family album is a prayer card that gives the date of his death as August 25, 1920. Photographs from the family album show him as a young man and on his wedding day. In another, he is standing in front of his bowling alley and saloon with his business associates. It was probably taken just a short time before his death.

71

Great-great-grandmother Nancy Wood Baker

FILLING OUT AN ANCESTOR CHART

You can use the information you have collected from family documents and interviews to fill out an ancestor or genealogical chart. Be sure to copy or photocopy the chart on the next page since you will probably need to use more than one copy.

If you feel uncomfortable working on your own genealogy, or simply can't find enough information about your family, you can still learn how to do family history. Try working on the genealogy of a famous historical figure or perhaps a prominent person in the history of your community.

Fill in the date and your name (as compiler) and address in the upper left-hand corner of the chart. Be sure to use a pencil. Number the chart "Ancestor Chart No. 1." Your name, or the name of the person you are working on, goes on line No. 1. Your father will be 2 and your mother 3. A father's number is always double that of his child while a mother's number is always double her child's, plus one.

You will be able to extend your genealogy by adding more Ancestor Charts. All the people listed on your No. 1 chart will always keep their original numbers. For example, your great-great-grandfather on line 16 on chart 1 will become 1 on chart 2. In the upper left-hand corner of chart 2 you will indicate that person 1 on this chart is the same person as 16 on chart 1. If you were to renumber chart 2 so that it becomes an extension of chart 1, the father of great-great-grandfather 16 would become 32. Always be sure to list a person's original number on any individual data sheets you fill out. This may sound a bit confusing at first, but it is really quite easy once you start doing it.

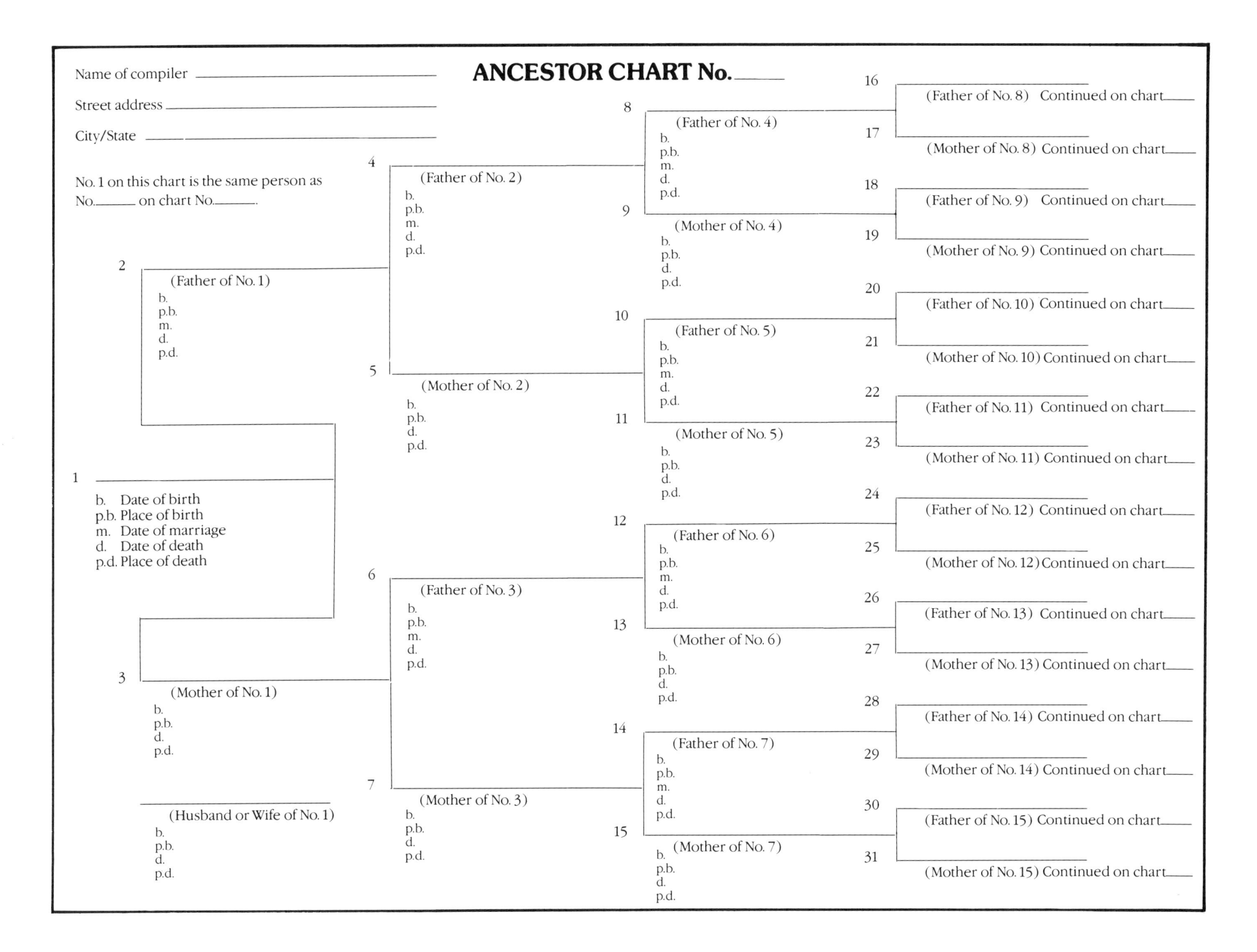

ANCESTOR CHART No.____

Name of compiler _____

Street address _____

City/State _____

No. 1 on this chart is the same person as
No.____ on chart No.____.

1 _____
- b. Date of birth
- p.b. Place of birth
- m. Date of marriage
- d. Date of death
- p.d. Place of death

2 (Father of No. 1)
- b.
- p.b.
- m.
- d.
- p.d.

3 (Mother of No. 1)
- b.
- p.b.
- d.
- p.d.

_____ (Husband or Wife of No. 1)
- b.
- p.b.
- d.
- p.d.

4 (Father of No. 2)
- b.
- p.b.
- m.
- d.
- p.d.

5 (Mother of No. 2)
- b.
- p.b.
- d.
- p.d.

6 (Father of No. 3)
- b.
- p.b.
- m.
- d.
- p.d.

7 (Mother of No. 3)
- b.
- p.b.
- d.
- p.d.

8 (Father of No. 4)
- b.
- p.b.
- m.
- d.
- p.d.

9 (Mother of No. 4)
- b.
- p.b.
- d.
- p.d.

10 (Father of No. 5)
- b.
- p.b.
- m.
- d.
- p.d.

11 (Mother of No. 5)
- b.
- p.b.
- d.
- p.d.

12 (Father of No. 6)
- b.
- p.b.
- m.
- d.
- p.d.

13 (Mother of No. 6)
- b.
- p.b.
- d.
- p.d.

14 (Father of No. 7)
- b.
- p.b.
- m.
- d.
- p.d.

15 (Mother of No. 7)
- b.
- p.b.
- d.
- p.d.

16 (Father of No. 8) Continued on chart____

17 (Mother of No. 8) Continued on chart____

18 (Father of No. 9) Continued on chart____

19 (Mother of No. 9) Continued on chart____

20 (Father of No. 10) Continued on chart____

21 (Mother of No. 10) Continued on chart____

22 (Father of No. 11) Continued on chart____

23 (Mother of No. 11) Continued on chart____

24 (Father of No. 12) Continued on chart____

25 (Mother of No. 12) Continued on chart____

26 (Father of No. 13) Continued on chart____

27 (Mother of No. 13) Continued on chart____

28 (Father of No. 14) Continued on chart____

29 (Mother of No. 14) Continued on chart____

30 (Father of No. 15) Continued on chart____

31 (Mother of No. 15) Continued on chart____

Copyright © 1984 by Addison-Wesley Publishing Company

> **We are the children of many sires, and every drop of blood in us in its turn betrays its ancestors.**

NAMES TELL STORIES TOO

As you find out more about your family's history, you will learn more about yourself and where you came from. The famous American poet and essayist Ralph Waldo Emerson (1803-1882) wrote: "We are the children of many sires, and every drop of blood in us in its turn betrays its ancestors."

Even your name has a whole story of its own. Take a close look at some of the names on your ancestor chart. Start with your own name. Were you named after anyone? If you were, what do you know about the relative or person for whom you were named?

Does your surname mean anything special? In Hispanic culture, if your surname is a name such as Garcia-Gomez, it is made up of your mother's maiden name (Garcia) and your father's name (Gomez).

Many surnames refer to specific trades and occupations. About seven hundred years ago, when communities became crowded enough that it was necessary to tell people apart, people started adopting surnames. Surnames were originally an extra name, or nickname, that made it easier to identify someone.

Often surnames were based upon places where people had their homes. Someone with the name Mary Hill probably had a distant relative who lived on or near a hill. Names like Forest and Wood, for example, came into being in much the same way. The Japanese name Yamashita means "one who lives below the mountain." A person whose surname is Forester probably has a distant relative who was a wood cutter or lumberjack.

Surnames based on occupations are extremely common. Names such as Baker, Miller, Chandler, Fletcher, and Smith are all based on the jobs of people in the past.

CHILDREN THEN AND NOW

Find a photograph of yourself taken when you were younger. Also try to find one of a grandparent or great-grandparent of the same sex and about the same age.

If you can't find two such photographs in your family album, study the two photographs of a grandmother and her granddaughter illustrated here.

Compare the clothing, hairstyles, and objects included in each photograph. Try to determine when and where each picture was taken. Are they both studio photographs or were they taken by someone in the family? What do the differences in the two photographs tell you about what it was like to be a child in the past compared to when you were younger?

Clara Levenia Martin Baker (1890-1972)

Asterie Patricia Baker (1948-   )

COMPARING HISTORICAL PHOTOGRAPHS FOR MORE INFORMATION

Photographs are often of greatest value to historians when they are compared with other photographs or with different kinds of evidence.

Look at the following three photographs of Pennsylvania Avenue, in Washington, D. C. They were all taken looking toward the Capitol from the steps of the Treasury Building. By closely studying these photographs, you can discover a lot about the history of this section of a famous street.

The earliest photograph dates from 1885. An iron fence encircles the lawn of the Treasury Building in the foreground. Horse-drawn carriages are moving down the street. People are also walking and riding horses on the street. The street itself seems very wide.

Several buildings are located in the left-hand corner of the picture, including the Solaris Hotel. If all you knew was that the photograph was taken in Washington, the name of the hotel might help you identify the street scene. You could look up the hotel in an old city directory to determine its address. If you needed to date the photograph, the Solaris Hotel might also be helpful.

There appear to be some residential buildings on the street, especially the second building from the front, right corner.

(Courtesy The National Archives.)

WHAT'S IN A NAME?

Included below is a list of English surnames based upon different crafts and trades. Many of them are similar to English words we use today. Check the names against similar words found in the dictionary. (By the way, special dictionaries of names such as Elston C. Smith's *Dictionary of American Family Names* can be found in most libraries.) Try to match each name with the trade or occupation it describes.

General William Sherman. Photograph by Mathew B. Brady. (Courtesy The National Archives.)

A. Chandler   ___ Arrow-maker

B. Fletcher   ___ Catcher of wild birds

C. Sherman   ___ Hawk or falcon trainer

D. Thatcher   ___ Candle-maker

E. Mason   ___ Wheel-maker, cart-maker, or carpenter

F. Byrd   ___ Cloth cutter

G. Clark   ___ Stone cutter

H. Faulkner   ___ Roofer

I. Tinker   ___ Scholar, clerk or records keeper

J. Wright   ___ Traveling salesman of pots, pans, and so forth

However, surnames today may not necessarily match the occupations of the people who bear them.

Raymond Chandler	writer
Louise Fletcher	actress
William Sherman	general
Margaret Thatcher	politican
James Mason	actor
Richard Byrd	explorer
William Clark	explorer
William Faulkner	author
Grant Tinker	producer
Wilbur and Orville Wright	aviators

Not just English surnames are based upon trades and occupations, or on the location of one's home. For example, Zimmermann means carpenter in German. The name is obviously Carpenter in English. Fischman is fish seller in German and corresponds to the English name of Fishman or Fisher. The occupation of smith (a metalworker such as a goldsmith or a blacksmith) is:

LeFever	in French
Schmidt	in German
Herrera	in Spanish
Haddad	in Arabic

Many times surnames are *patronymics* or names received from paternal ancestors (ancestors on the father's side). These are formed with a prefix or suffix as in *Fitz*gerald (son of Gerald), or Robert*son* (son of Robert). Prefixes and suffixes are used in patronymics in many languages:

English	son	John*son*
French	de	*de* Maurier
Chinese	tse	Lao*tse*
Hebrew	ben	*ben*-Gurion
Spanish	es, ez	Gom*ez*
German	sohn	*Sohn*heim
Greek	poulos	Pado*poulos*

Der Schmidt.

Der Goldtschmid.

Robert of Nowhere in Particular

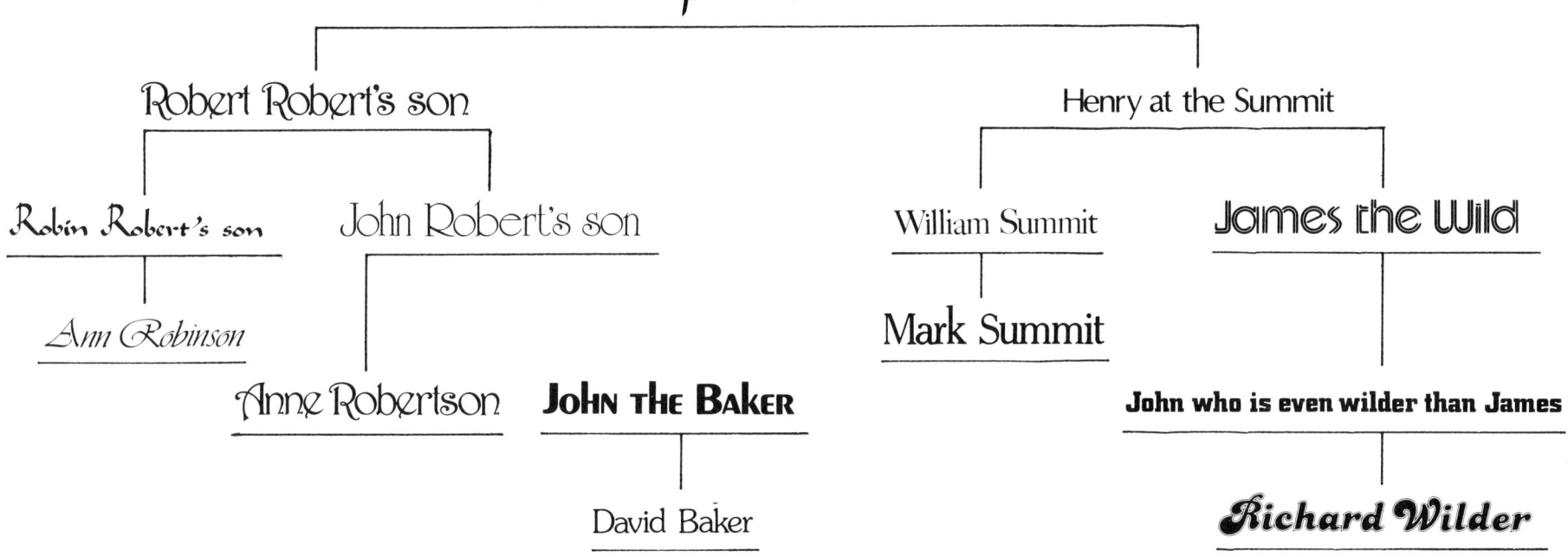

Robert Robert's son
- Robin Robert's son
  - Ann Robinson
- John Robert's son
  - Anne Robertson
  - John the Baker
    - David Baker

Henry at the Summit
- William Summit
  - Mark Summit
- James the Wild
  - John who is even wilder than James
    - Richard Wilder

Sometimes a patronymic suffix is added to a nickname. Robin is the nickname for Robert, so Robertson became Robinson.

When you look at your ancestor chart, you may notice that surnames have been used as given names, or first names, to perpetuate the surname.

In many families certain given names have been used over and over. In earlier times when many children died in childhood, the same name was given to more than one child of the same sex in a family. The parents were trying to insure that at least one child with the name would survive.

In many early German families, all the boy children were given their father's name and all the girls were named after their mother. Many given names, such as Ashley, Marie, Lee, and even June, have been used for both sexes.

Sometimes names tell you something about what the person was like as a baby. In Swahili, the name Kifimbo means a very thin baby. In Twi, the language of Ghana, the name Kunto means a female, third child. In Arabic, the name Lateefah means a gentle, pleasant, female child.

Many names are also spelled in several different ways, even within the same family. Therefore, when you are searching for your ancestors in indexes and public records, always be sure to check every possible spelling and variation of a name.

You may also notice changes in spelling from one generation to the next. Or you may discover changes in surnames among your ancestors. When many of your ancestors immigrated to the United States, they changed their names. If they had no surname, they often adopted a patronymical name. Perhaps their name was translated into English, such as Cohn into King. Or a prefix or suffix was dropped. They may even have adopted a completely new name.

In discovering more about your family history you may find out that a member of your family used one surname in the English-speaking community and was known by another in his or her own family or ethnic community.

USING ARCHIVES, LIBRARIES, AND GOVERNMENT RECORDS TO TRACE YOUR FAMILY'S HISTORY

In tracing your ancestors, you will also learn a lot about geography and history. Why did they come to the United States, for example? Were they immigrating because of religious persecution or political oppression? Did they come for economic reasons? Were they brought to this country against their will?

In his book *Roots*, Alex Haley uses his family's history as the basis of a detailed historical novel. He begins the book with the capture of one of his relatives in Africa, hundreds of years ago. The story continues into the twentieth century with his own life.

Haley began his novel one day in 1965. Out of curiosity, he walked into the genealogical records division of the National Archives in Washington, D.C. There he was able to begin to verify stories that had been handed down to him orally by his grandmother.

In researching your own family's history, you will eventually run out of people to interview, old family photograph albums, and documents. In order to continue, you will have to begin to work in public libraries and archives.

Many public libraries and historical associations have special local history and genealogy collections. These collections typically include:

    newspaper clippings

    extracts or abstracts or real estate and probate records

    city directories

    old telephone directories

    catalogs of cemetery markers

    maps

    state, county, and town records

    country and state histories and atlases

Hymeneal.

Married, at South Fork in Pettis county, at 8 o'clock Wednesday. the 16th inst., C. B. Martin, of Saline, to Carrie E. Spurgeon, of Pettis W. N. Phillips officiating.

The ushers were Messrs. Bright, J. Hammock, J. R. Ph and W. S. Holmes, and a l number of relatives and fri witnessed the ceremony.

The groom is one of Sali most worthy citizens, an int gent, industrious and deserv young man, and the bride one Pettis county's fairest and m accomplished daughters.

Baker Services To Be Friday

June Baker, 81, passed away Tuesday at his farm near Napton.

Funeral services will be at 3:30 p.m. Friday at the Smith-Chapel Methodist Church with Rev. David Wendleton, pastor, officiating. Burial will be in the Smith Chapel Cemetery. Campbell-Lewis Funeral Home is in charge.

The family will be at the church after one o'clock Friday.

CHARLES N. MARTIN

es at the Advanced age of Ninety-one Years.

At his home six miles south-st of Marshall, Charles N. artin, died Saturday night, eb. 10th, at the age of 91 years. otwithstanding the fact that he old gentleman had lived almost a century and had been feeble for several years on account of his age, his general health was good up to Thursday of last week he was stricken with a cold,

---

LT. SPROW, WAR PRISONER, GETS SERVICE HONORS

Reported Missing

LT. W. J. "SUNNY" SPROW

Second Lieut. W. J. "Sunny" Sprow, reported by the War Department as missing in action over Europe since Oct. 10, is believed to have participated in raids over the German transportation centers of Muenster and Coesfeld which

---

Most librarians will be interested in helping you with your family history research. However, it is not their job to do research for you. Try to discover as much as you can on your own before asking for their help. You need to have a clear idea of what you are looking for.

For example, you may know that one of your great-grandfathers was born in Steubenville, Ohio, sometime in the early 1890s. If you don't know exactly when, try to guess at the date. Then start looking through sources such as birth announcements in the Steubenville newspapers. Or look in the records of births included in local or county records.

You may want to request materials from one of the major genealogical libraries in the country. These include:

The National Archives and
  Record Services, NNC
Washington, D. C. 20408

The Library of
  The Church of Jesus Christ
  of Latter Day Saints
50 East North Temple Street
Salt Lake City, Utah 84150

which has 235 branches throughout the world.

To use federal records, you must know an ancestor's name, where and when he or she lived, and how he or she worked with or served the federal government.

Many local public libraries have bibliographies and indexes of genealogies that have already been printed as books or articles in magazines.

USING BIRTH, MARRIAGE, AND DEATH CERTIFICATES TO TRACE YOUR FAMILY'S HISTORY

In conducting your family history research, you will develop many of the skills of a professional historian. You will search different sources and compare them in order to determine the accuracy of their data. You will use various references and indexes and develop many problem-solving skills as well.

Other sources you may wish to study include birth, marriage, and death certificates. These are usually filed in the office of the city or town clerk who has jurisdiction over the place where the event took place.

Death certificates, for example, will tell you the name, date, and place of birth of the deceased, as well as the date and cause of death. They may also include the names and birthplaces of the deceased person's father and mother. Also look at cemetery records and funeral director's records. Check the obituary notices in old newspapers.

Probate records are an assortment of documents that were used to complete the process of settling the real (real estate) and personal estate of a deceased person. Check out where they are located in your town (usually in the courthouse). You can use an *Index to Administrations and Estates* to help you locate the records of members of your family.

Probate records describe the distribution of the deceased person's estate. They also provide lists of heirs, spouses, sons, and daughters, including their married names and current addresses. Probate records include other documents besides wills, such as:

- guardianship papers
- adoption proceedings
- delayed birth certificates
- changes of names
- records of secret marriages

You can gain access to many other records in local, state, and federal archives by visiting your courthouse. Land records include deeds, mortgages, leases, maps, and plats. You can track down registers of voters, coroner's files, and naturalization records.

You can also obtain many records by writing to the clerk of the court. Be sure your written request for information is short and concise. It must include an exact description of the type of information you are searching for.

USING THE FEDERAL CENSUS RECORDS TO TRACE YOUR FAMILY'S HISTORY

The federal census or local censuses conducted by schools, cities, and counties may also provide you with important information on your family. From 1600 to 1789, some censuses were taken in the American colonies under the supervision of colonial governors.

The first federal census was taken in 1790, and one has been taken every ten years since then. As specified in Article One of the Constitution, the federal census is taken for the purpose of determining how many representatives in Congress each state is entitled to have, based upon its population.

In 1790 it was very hard to find *enumerators* or people to take or record the census. The pay was very low and no paper forms were provided. It is said that a part of that census was recorded on wallpaper! The first federal census recorded:

- name of the head of the family
- number of free white males over sixteen years of age
- number of free white males under sixteen years of age
- number of free white females
- number of free black persons
- number of slaves

As you can see, the 1790 census did not distinguish between the number of people in the family and those in the household.

The 1850 census was the first to record all the names of the persons in a household. But many people considered the questions on the census too personal, so they provided inaccurate information.

The federal censuses from 1790 to 1890 that have survived (more than 90 percent of the 1890 census was destroyed by fire in 1921) are available on microfilm in many libraries throughout the country.

USING PASSENGER ARRIVAL LISTS TO TRACE YOUR FAMILY'S HISTORY

In tracking down immigrant ancestors it may be helpful to look at passenger arrival lists compiled by ship captains, which go back as far as 1798. Many of these lists are on microfilm in the National Archives. They are difficult to search, though. For example, one year before the Civil War the lists recorded that more than 300,000 people arrived in the United States. You will need to know the name of the port of entry, the name of the ship, and as exact an arrival date for the ship as possible.

When you search through old documents and records, try to remember not to impose today's meaning or your own interpretation on the dates or events of another period.

If you don't understand a word that you come across or the way it is used in one of the documents, even in an old letter, it might be helpful to look up the word in a dictionary from the same period as the document.

"Steerage" by Alfred Steiglitz, 1907. (Courtesy The Library of Congress.

USEFUL TERMS IN STUDYING FAMILY HISTORY AND GENEALOGY

There will be many legal terms used on documents that you may not know. We have included definitions of some of these terms as well as some terms of kinship that might be a bit confusing.

ANCESTOR: Person from whom another is descended in direct line.

ATTEST: To give proof or certify that something is true or correct.

BANNS: The spoken or written notice, given three separate times, that a certain man and woman are to be married.

BOUNTY: Money paid by a city or town to volunteers for army service as an inducement to serve.

BOUNTY LAND: Land given by the government as a bounty.

BROTHER/SISTER: Son or daughter of the same parents. Sometimes used for a close friend or member of the same union, club, religious organization, and so on.

BROTHER-IN-LAW/SISTER-IN-LAW: Brother or sister of one's husband or wife, or husband or wife of one's brother or sister.

CENSUS: An official count of the people of a district, state, or country.

CODICIL: Supplement to a will.

COLLATERAL ANCESTOR: Secondary relative such as the brother of a direct ancestor, but not in a direct line of descent.

CONSANGUINEOUS: Of the same blood. Descended from the same ancestor.

COUSIN: Son or daughter of one's uncle or aunt. In seventeenth-century wills, a cousin is any relative not a brother or sister, son or daughter. Therefore, a grandchild might be called a cousin.

DAUGHTER-IN-LAW/SON-IN-LAW: Husband or wife of one's child. In the seventeenth century, step-children might also be called daughter-in-law or son-in-law.

DECEDENT: Dead person.

DECLARATION OF INTENTION: The first paper or sworn statement made by an alien who intends to become a citizen.

DENIZEN: Person admitted to residence in a foreign country and permitted certain rights of citizenship.

DOWER: A widow's share for life of her dead husband's property.

DESC.: Descendant.

EMIGRANT: Person who leaves his or her own country to settle in another.

EXECUTOR: Person named in a will to carry out the wishes of the person making the will.

FEE SIMPLE: Land of which the inheritor has unqualified ownership.

FEE TAIL: Land the inheritance of which is limited to particular heirs.

FREEMAN: Person who was not a slave and held full rights of citizenship and could vote and enter into business arrangements.

GENEALOGY: Account of the descent of a person or family from an ancestor or ancestors. From two Greek words meaning birth and study.

GENTLEMAN: Man of "gentle birth" (descendant of an aristocratic family), whose income is obtained from the rental of his lands.

GOODMAN/GOODWIFE: Man or his spouse who is a respected and substantial member of the community.

GRANTOR: Person who gives or sells real estate.

HOLOGRAPHIC WILL: A handwritten will.

IMMIGRANT: Person who comes to a country to live there.

INDENTURE: Contract by which a person is bound to serve someone else.

INDENTURED SERVANT: A person who bound himself or herself for a number of years to pay a debt, often for passage to America. Originally, indenture documents were cut or torn apart leaving a notched edge. The genuineness of the document could be proved at any time by matching up the edges. In this sense, one was said to "indent" the contract.

INFANT: Any person under legal age.

INTESTATE: Having died without leaving a will.

JUNIOR/SENIOR: Not necessarily father and son — might be younger and older person with the same name living in the same area.

KINDRED: Relatives by blood.

LEGACY: Bequest of money or other property left by the last will and testament of someone who has died.

LINEAGE: Descent in direct line from a common ancestor.

LINEAL ANCESTOR: Direct ancestor.

MIGRATION: Movement from one residence to another, usually from one part of the country to another.

MR.: Title put before a man's name or the name of his office, as in Mr. President. In early colonial days it was used only for those who held important civil office or were of gentle blood.

MRS.: Title put in front of a married woman's name. However, in the seventeenth and eighteenth centuries it was an abbreviation of Mistress, which was used for an unmarried woman.

N.D.: No date.

NEE: Born. Placed after the name of a married woman to show her maiden name, as in Clara Baker, nee Martin.

NONCUPATIVE WILL: An oral will made before witnesses (often a deathbed will) and later written down by someone other than the testator.

PATENT: Conveyance of land title by a government.

PATENTEE: Person who receives a land title from a government.

PATRONYMIC: A name received from a paternal ancestor. From the Latin word *patronymicus*, which means "derived from the name of the father."

PEDIGREE: Recorded line of descent. From the old French words *pie de grue*, or "crane's foot," after the three-line, claw-shaped mark that was used to show descent on early genealogical charts.

POSTHUMOUS: Occuring after a person's death.

PROGENITORS: Ancestors in direct line.

QUANTITATIVE HISTORY: History that uses numbers to make new discoveries about the past.

REDEMPTIONER: Person who paid for his or her passage by becoming an indentured servant.

RELICT: Usually a widow.

UNM: Unmarried.

UXOR: Wife.

TESTATOR: Person who has/had made a valid will before their death.

WID.: Widow, woman whose husband is dead and who has not married again.

WIDR.: Widower, man whose wife is dead and who has not married again.

WILL: Legal statement or document in which a person tells what is to be done with his or her property after death.

QUANTITATIVE FAMILY HISTORY

You can use the vital statistics and numbers you have gathered for your family history as the basis for some interesting comparisons between the different generations in your family. By counting and tabulating many of the dates in your genealogy, you can come up with some interesting family history.

For example, compute the age at death of all the women in your family and all of the men. Total up the ages for each sex and determine the average age of death for each sex. Which sex seems to live longer?

You could also find the average age of death for each generation, such as your great-grandparents and your great-great-grandparents. Compare these averages to determine if there are any significant differences in average life-spans between generations.

Quantitative history can also be used to study the sizes of families in your genealogy. Determine the family size for each of your four sets of great-grandparents. Also determine the family size and the average for your two sets of grandparents or your eight sets of great-great-grandparents. How do these figures compare? How do the averages compare? Has the size of families changed? If there have been changes, what has caused these changes?

Quantitative methods for family history do not have to be concerned simply with deaths and the sizes of families. You can also compute:

How many times families have moved.

How many members entered what professions.

How much education family members had.

How old they were when they got married.

How old the women were when they had their first child.

You can see how the dates and numbers in your genealogy can be used to provide you with some quantitative history. Quantitative history can also tell you a lot about patterns in your own family and how they compare to general trends in the society. You may find it interesting to compare your results with those of a friend who is also working on a family history.

Family history provides many different opportunities to study the past. You also get to learn how to use many different types of historical documents and discover new ways of doing research. You may decide to write a biographical sketch of a relative; the history of a family business; the history of your family as newly arrived immigrants in this country; of their travels throughout the United States; or the history of a family member's military career.

It is important to remember that your history and the history of your family is part of a much larger history — not only American but even world history. Don't forget that history begins at home! And the events in your life today will become tomorrow's family history.

SPRIGG
NOV. 18, 1870
JAN. 1, 1956
MARTIN
E. CAROLINE
JULY 7, 1866
MAY 19, 1947
J. C. BRACK
JULY 25, 1864
BAKER
AND THREE INFANTS
WIFE

CEMETERIES

Chapter 4: CEMETERIES

A cemetery can be one of the most fascinating and richest sources of historical information in your town. It can provide you with information about some of the famous, even notorious, people who have lived in your community. And if you are lucky and live in the same town as some of your ancestors, it may give you some clues about your own history.

Cemeteries can also provide clues to some of the important events in the history of your community. For example, you may find that many people died in a certain year because of an epidemic or because of a natural disaster such as a flood. You can discover how your community has grown by mapping the different locations of the cemeteries.

Cemeteries are really unlike any other place in the world. How do you feel about them? Do you avoid them because they scare you? Or because they make you think about things, like death, that you would just as soon not think about? Maybe you feel a deep respect for cemeteries and for the people who are buried in them.

The different cemeteries in your community can tell you a lot about the people who have lived there as well as something about where they came from and their personal lives and attitudes. All you have to do is learn to decode the messages that cemeteries and their tombstones and monuments have preserved for you.

Perhaps you will even find that you like visiting cemeteries. You may become fascinated by the tombstones — by their sculpture, symbols, and the epitaphs engraved on them.

A plaque commemorating the Austins in a cemetery in Durham, Connecticut, and two of the family's houses still standing in town.

89

INVENTORY OF THE CEMETERIES IN YOUR COMMUNITY

Perhaps one of the best ways to begin to use cemeteries as sources of historical data is to make an inventory of all of the cemeteries you can find in your community. You may already know about many of them or members of your family may help you make your list.

Another source is your city telephone directory. The yellow pages should have a listing under "Cemeteries and Memorial Parks."

List on a chart all of the cemeteries you can find. You can trace or photocopy as many copies of the chart included in this book as you need. Include:

The name of the cemetery.

Its location and address.

Whether it is connected with a particular religion.

Any other information you find out about it.

If you wish, you can locate all of the graveyards on your inventory list on a map of your town or region.

By mapping your community's cemeteries, you should be able to discover how your town has grown. Are these cemeteries in or next to city parks? Have they been surrounded by buildings and neighborhoods as your town has built up? Are certain types of cemeteries located in particular areas of town?

If you live in a rural area, you can map the church and family cemeteries in your county. You may discover that some of these were originally on farms or in towns and churchyards that have disappeared or been abandoned. You may even discover a few lost or forgotten cemeteries!

DIFFERENT TYPES OF CEMETERIES

The very earliest cemeteries in the United States probably were mass graves without any tombstones. During the 1600s, many people died of epidemics, starvation, and in hostilities with the Indians. The early settlers simply did not have the time or materials to build enough cemeteries and tombstones.

In New England, when simple wooden markers could be constructed or stone markers carved, they usually reflected the Puritans' attitudes about death, and the hardships of early colonial life. The markers and their messages were reminders to the living that life is short and that death is the time of judgment for all of us. For this reason, the cemeteries were usually near the centers of towns. They might be next to meeting houses, churches, or town

---

**Behold my friends as you pass by
As you are now so once was I
As I am now, so you must be
Prepare for death and follow me.**

buildings. Cemeteries were a very important part of the town and everyone's day-to-day lives.

In many rural areas of the country, families had their own cemeteries. These plots are particularly interesting because they usually include the graves of several generations of the same family. Some families even have cemeteries for their favorite animals and pets.

>Erected to the
>Memory of
>Old Blue
>The Best Cowpony
>That Ever Pulled
>A Rope
>by the Cowpunchers
>of the
>7XL
>Outfit
>Rest in Peace

— Warren Ranch, near Cheyenne, Wyoming

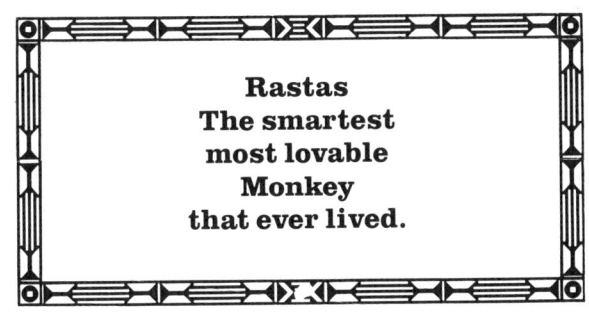

>**Rastas**
>**The smartest**
>**most lovable**
>**Monkey**
>**that ever lived.**

— Canine Cemetery, Hartsdale, New York

Photograph by Michael L. Carlebach

Rural churches also often have their own cemeteries where members of the church and several generations of the same family may be buried. Church cemeteries are usually smaller than other types of graveyards.

Your community may have some special cemeteries, such as a military cemetery commemorating American soldiers from a particular war. These cemeteries may be in parks by themselves or located on a military base.

As more and more people moved to the cities, the churchyard cemeteries became overcrowded. Therefore, many towns established *detached cemeteries*. They were usually built in a natural landscape setting on the outskirts of the town, detached from any particular church or public building.

Many of the detached cemeteries are surrounded by wrought-iron fences or walls of stone to protect them. They often have huge gates. Grove Street Cemetery in New Haven, Connecticut, has a massive Egyptian Revival gate.

Some of these cemeteries have avenues and paths that are laid out in a rigid grid pattern. In others, like Bellefontaine Cemetery in St. Louis, Missouri, the lanes gently curve around the trees and small hills. The avenues themselves are often named after trees, shrubs, and flowers.

The grounds of these cemeteries are usually well-landscaped. Sometimes they even have lakes and ponds. You may find that some of these cemeteries are really gardens and bird sanctuaries, tucked away within cities. Some, like the Trinity Churchyard in New York City, which is no longer used as a graveyard, are used as parks by the people in the neighborhood. Pieces of cemetery furniture, such as benches, provide the visitors with a quiet place to rest, nestled amid the hustle and bustle of the city.

Many detached cemeteries have office buildings, chapels and shelters for visitors in bad weather. Large mausoleums, smaller tombs, and graves marked with gravestones provide resting places for the dead.

VISITING CEMETERIES

Cemeteries are also places for the living to visit. Some of them have been designed as the scene for great processional funerals. In the past, cemeteries were considered an ideal place to promenade. People spent Sunday afternoons strolling about, admiring the monuments and picnicking.

Other people may go to a cemetery on a pilgrimage to the grave of a famous person. Or they may go to pay homage to the dead. Cemeteries are also wonderful places for being alone to contemplate.

Whenever you go to a cemetery, you should show the proper respect to the dead and their final resting place. Do not walk over the burial mounds themselves, if you can help it. Usually, there are paths between rows of graves that you can follow. Always try to approach headstones from the side instead of stepping directly on the grave mound.

You may meet other people in the cemetery. They may be there to search for the grave of a famous person, to make a tombstone rubbing, or to pay their respects to a dead relative or friend. They may enjoy talking with you. On the other hand, they may want to be left alone. Respect their right to privacy and quiet and move on to another part of the cemetery.

MAKING A SITE MAP OF A CEMETERY

You may find that it is a lot easier to get to know a cemetery by studying how it is designed. Almost all cemeteries provide maps for visitors. But if a cemetery you like does not have a map, you can draw your own. If the cemetery is really large, you may want to focus on just one section of it.

Describe the location of the cemetery within your town or county. What condition is it in? Can you visit it at any time or do you need to be specially admitted?

Look at how the lanes and avenues are laid out. Is the cemetery designed for pedestrians only or can automobiles drive through it? What are the lanes' names? Label the lanes on your map with their correct names.

Are there any family plots? How can you identify them? Are they protected by fences? How large are they? Be sure that these plots are marked on your map.

Check to see if there are any buildings in the cemetery, such as a chapel or a shelter for visitors in bad weather. Show these buildings on your map. How do they compare with the cemetery wall or fence? Can you tell if all the buildings were built at the same time?

Is there any cemetery furniture? Where is it? Are pieces such as benches placed next to certain tombs or perhaps by a lake?

Also mark some of your favorite tombs or some of the oldest ones on your map. Make any special notes that will help you find some of the most interesting tombs when you return to the cemetery.

SOURCES OF HISTORICAL INFORMATION IN CEMETERIES

Within the cemetery itself, the most obvious sources of historical information are the mausoleums, tombstones, and gravemarkers themselves. Tombs and memorial markers have been used for thousands of years by every culture. They have been constructed in almost every conceivable shape and size.

The ancient Egyptian pyramids are famous examples. Careful study of their design and construction can tell us a great deal about how much the ancient Egyptians knew about stonecutting and engineering. By examining the remains and artifacts included inside the tombs themselves, an entire culture can be revealed to us.

> In memory of Oliver Bacon, Son of Lieu.t Oliver & Mrs Rebecca Bacon who was killed by lightning July 2nd 1801. aged 8 Years. & 7 months.

— Jaffrey, New Hampshire

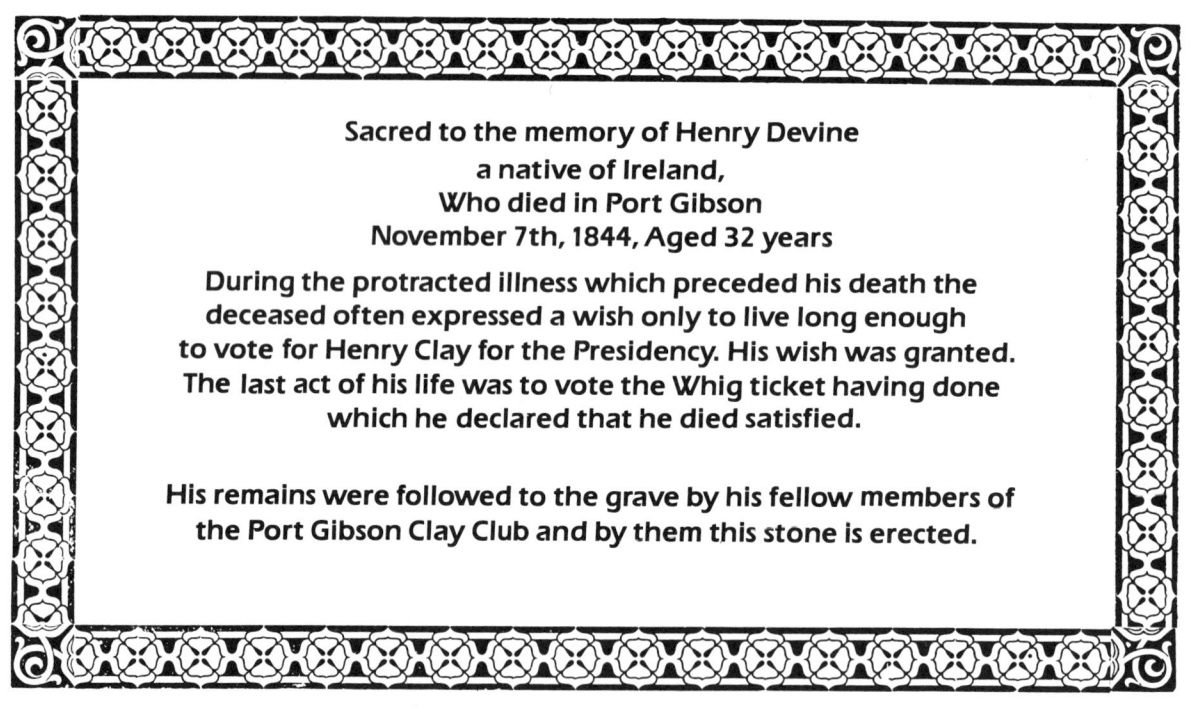

> Sacred to the memory of Henry Devine
> a native of Ireland,
> Who died in Port Gibson
> November 7th, 1844, Aged 32 years
>
> During the protracted illness which preceded his death the deceased often expressed a wish only to live long enough to vote for Henry Clay for the Presidency. His wish was granted. The last act of his life was to vote the Whig ticket having done which he declared that he died satisfied.
>
> His remains were followed to the grave by his fellow members of the Port Gibson Clay Club and by them this stone is erected.

— Tombstone in Wintergreen Cemetery, Port Gibson, Mississippi

Portrait brasses placed over graves in the Middle Ages are another example of famous tomb markers. By looking at these monumental brasses, the historian can uncover information about metallurgy and engraving techniques during the Middle Ages. You can learn a great deal about clothing, armor, and costume design. They also tell us about the history of the person being memorialized.

The inscriptions and epitaphs on the tombstones in the cemeteries in your community can provide you with all sorts of fascinating information about your community and the people who have lived there. The inscriptions may give you facts and dates such as people's names, and their birth and death dates.

The epitaphs may tell you much more about what people did in their lives; what their attitudes about death were; and what other people thought about them.

The decorations of the tombstones themselves can also tell you something about the people buried there and about the culture when they lived. For example, the tomb of Captain Isaiah Sellers in Bellefontaine Cemetery in St. Louis, Missouri, has a bas-relief carving of Sellers standing at the wheel of his boat. Sellers was a familiar steamboat captain on the Mississippi River between St. Louis and New Orleans. He was the first person to use the pseudonym Mark Twain. This was the same name that the famous humorist, novelist, and former riverboat pilot Samuel L. Clemens used as his pen name.

All of this type of information is part of the message the dead person leaves behind for people just like you to read. Sometimes, though, you may have to "decode" the messages on the tombstones to really understand what is being said.

READING GRAVESTONES AND EPITAPHS

Gravestones are really artifacts of our past and present culture and are important primary sources. They are packed full of all sorts of historical information for you to discover. It may be easiest to begin by decoding the written information on the tombstones.

For example, look at the five tombstones and epitaphs shown here and on the next page. Try to read them to discover the names of the persons they commemorate. Find out when they were born and when they died. Discover the names of other people related to the deceased and how they are related.

You may find that tombstones carved before the late 1800s do not give the date of the person's birth. Instead, they may tell you the date of death and that the person died in a specific year of their life. You will have to be careful with your math in figuring their year of birth.

For example, a tombstone may tell you that a person died on March 1, 1856, aged fifty-six. If his birthday was before or on March 1, then he was born in 1800 and would have turned fifty-six years old before his death. But if his birthday was after March 1st, he would have been born in 1799 but still would have been aged fifty-six at the time of his death because he would not have had his fifty-seventh birthday yet.

Usually tombstones carved after the late 1800s give you both the dates of birth and death, if they are known. But if this information is not shown you may have to list the year of birth as 1799/1800, for example.

— Provincetown, Massachusetts

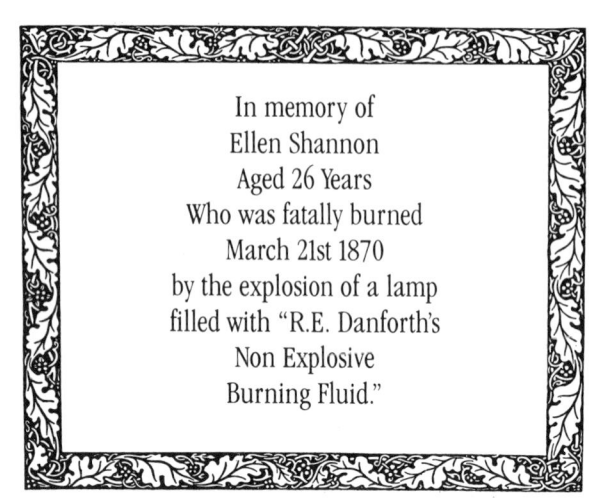

In memory of
Ellen Shannon
Aged 26 Years
Who was fatally burned
March 21st 1870
by the explosion of a lamp
filled with "R.E. Danforth's
Non Explosive
Burning Fluid."

— Girard, Pennsylvania

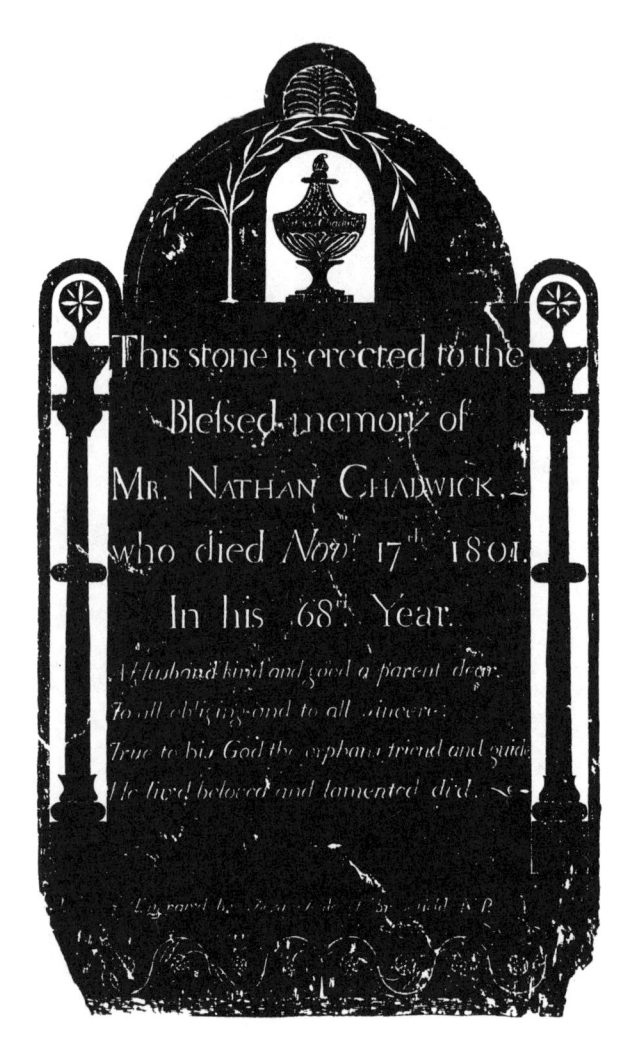

This stone is erected to the
Blessed memory of
Mr. NATHAN CHADWICK
who died Nov. 17th 1801.
In his 68th Year.

A Husband kind and good a parent dear
To all obliging and to all sincere
True to his God the orphans friend and guide
He lived beloved and lamented died.

— Warren, Massachusetts

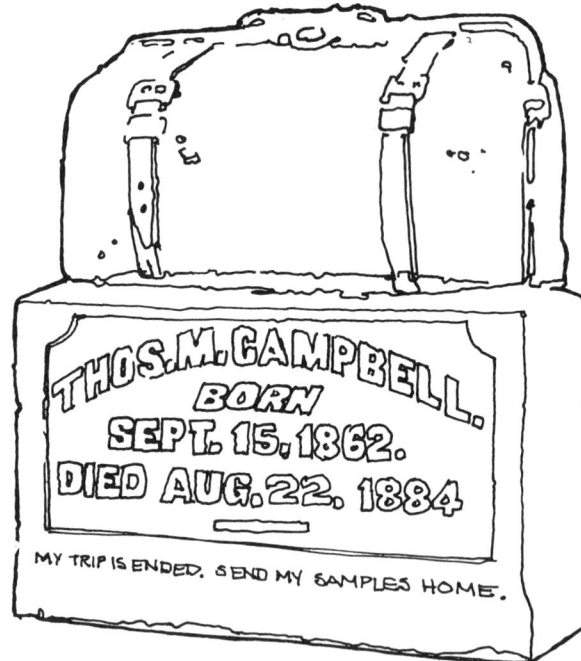

THOS. M. CAMPBELL.
BORN
SEPT. 15, 1862.
DIED AUG. 22, 1884

MY TRIP IS ENDED. SEND MY SAMPLES HOME.

— Burlington, Iowa

DEPOSITED
Beneath this Stone the Mortal Part
of Mrs. Susanna Jayne, the amiable Wife of
Mr. Peter Jayne, who lived Beloved
and Died Universally Lamented, on
August 8th 1776 in the 45th
Year of her Age.

— Marblehead, Massachusetts

John Hancock

Paul Revere

Samuel Adams

A WALK THROUGH HISTORY

As you learn to read the messages left in cemeteries you will begin to understand that a walk through a cemetery can be a walk through history. Sometimes you only have to read the names on the tombstones to appreciate this sense of history.

For example, in the Granary Burying Ground in Boston, you would come across the graves of John Hancock (1737-1793); Samual Adams (1722-1803); Paul Revere (1735-1818); and Mary Goose (died October 9, 1690), author of the Mother Goose nursery rhymes.

A walk through a family cemetery, or even a family plot in a larger cemetery, often helps people interested in family history compile quite a lot of data about their family. Until the mid-1900s, many families lived in the same region for several generations and were buried together. Therefore, a trip to a cemetery may provide new information about a family. Or it might verify dates and names from other sources, or even provide a missing link in the family history.

HOW TO READ INSCRIPTIONS

You will find that in many old cemeteries you must really study the stones carefully. Worn and weathered inscriptions are sometimes very hard to read. You may find it helpful to shade the stone so that the sun doesn't throw such deep shadows over its face. Or you can use a piece of white chalk to trace the inscription and make it easier to read.

Whenever you copy inscriptions and epitaphs from gravestones it is important to copy them word by word and letter for letter. Also include all punctuation marks. If some letters are impossible to read, you should enclose what you think the missing letter or word is in parentheses:

(H)annah, Wife of
(Jere)miah B. Johnson

If you have been able to visit a cemetery you have probably noticed an amazing variety of first names on the tombstones. Some may be names you have read in books or heard on television. Others may seem completely foreign to you. Perhaps they are very old and were popular a long time ago.

In fact, by comparing names and dates you will probably find that certain names were very popular during particular periods in the past, just as others are today.

It is interesting to see how many sons are named for their fathers. You will probably find that very few daughters are named for their mothers.

Maybe some names you find are even part of an inscription written in a foreign language. Many of these tombstones are a record of the immigration of the people they commemorate. The language inscribed on the gravestones may help you determine a person's ethnic heritage. You may even run across some languages you have never seen before.

Many stones also tell you the country of birth of the immigrants. By studying the dates on these gravestones, you may find that several people from the same country came to the region together. Such information can help you learn a lot about the ethnic history of your town.

You will also probably notice that many people were born in another part of the country and moved to your region. Perhaps members of the same family came to your region together or even several families may have come at the same time.

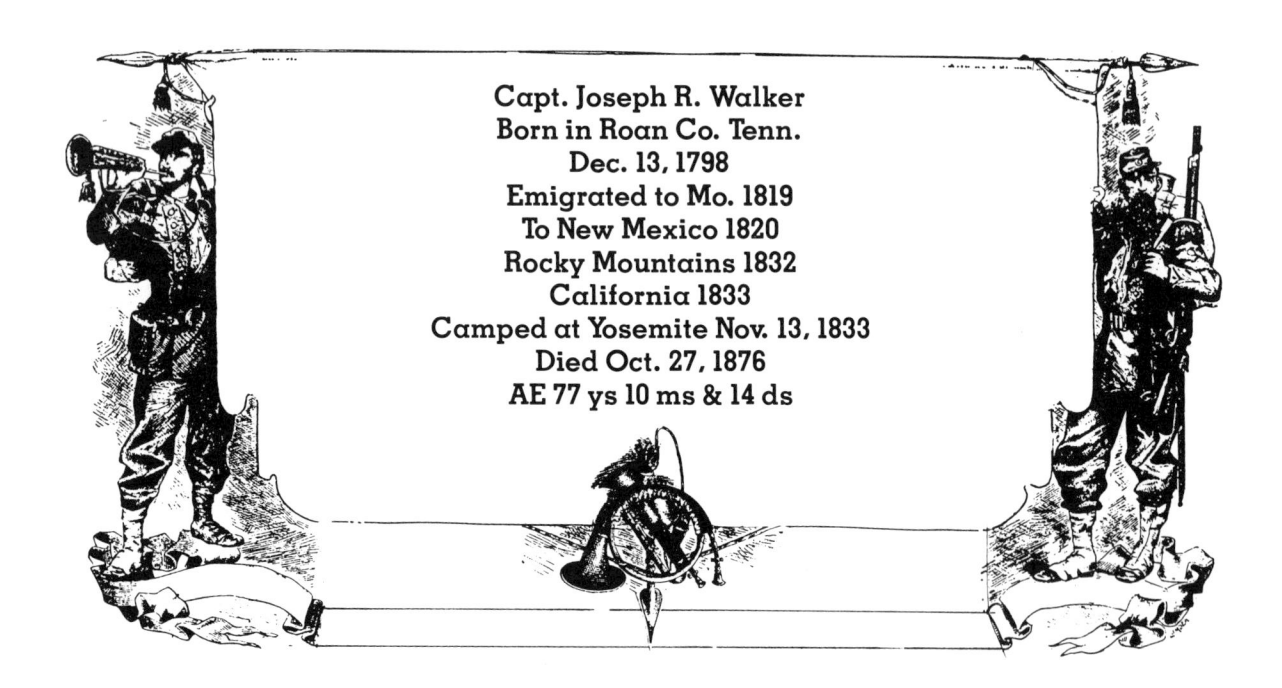

Capt. Joseph R. Walker
Born in Roan Co. Tenn.
Dec. 13, 1798
Emigrated to Mo. 1819
To New Mexico 1820
Rocky Mountains 1832
California 1833
Camped at Yosemite Nov. 13, 1833
Died Oct. 27, 1876
AE 77 ys 10 ms & 14 ds

— Alhambra Cemetery, Martinez, California

CEMETERY CENSUS

A cemetery is a great place to study the ethnic background and history of your community. You can trace or photocopy as many copies of the chart included in this book as you need for your cemetery census. List all the different countries of birth found on the tombstones in a cemetery in your town. Record how many people were born in each of these countries. You may also be able to list towns and states of the United States. Try to notice if more people seem to have been born in certain regions.

Tombstones inscribed in foreign languages also provide clues to the ethnic history of your region. Try to discover what these languages are. Do they help you determine the person's place of origin? List the foreign languages used in the cemetery. Note how many tombstones are inscribed with each language.

People's last names or surnames may also give you a clue to their ethnic background, the country of their birth, or where their parents were from. Copy down all the interesting surnames you can find. Use a reference book on surnames from a library to help you determine the ethnic origin of the names. Keep track of how many people had the same surname.

Use the information you have gathered from the tombstone inscriptions to try to describe the ethnic history of the cemetery you have visited. You should also be able to draw some conclusions about the ethnic history of your town or region.

EPITAPHS: MESSAGES FROM THE DEAD

While visiting a cemetery you will probably notice that there are many different kinds of epitaphs inscribed on the tombstones and monuments. Sometimes these verses and sayings tell you something about the deceased person. Other times they may tell you more about the culture of our country.

For example, one of the most treasured epitaphs in the United States is in Arlington National Cemetery. It is on the Tomb of the Unknown Soldier of World War I:

> **Here Rests in
> Honored Glory
> An American
> Soldier
> Known But to God**

This epitaph honors the memory of all the unknown and lost soldiers of the War who died for our country.

Many other epitaphs commemorate an heroic deed of the deceased person so that they will not be forgotten. A tombstone in Copp's Hill Burying Ground in Boston records for history the deed of a man who helped the American fight for independence:

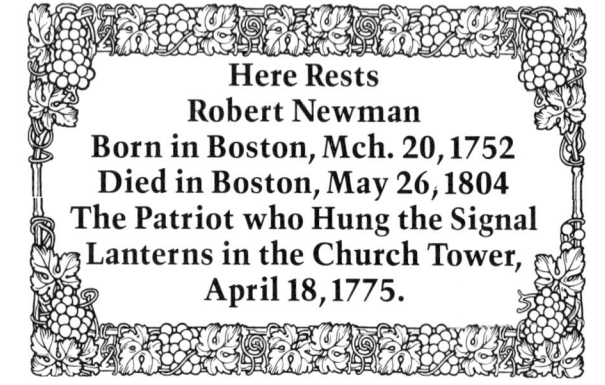

> **Here Rests
> Robert Newman
> Born in Boston, Mch. 20, 1752
> Died in Boston, May 26, 1804
> The Patriot who Hung the Signal
> Lanterns in the Church Tower,
> April 18, 1775.**

Some epitaphs record how a person died, sometimes heroically:

> **In honored memory of
> Sarah J. Rooke
> Telephone Operator
> Who perished in the flood
> waters of the Dry Cimarron
> at Folsom, New Mexico, August
> 27, 1908 while at her switch-
> board warning others of the
> danger. With heroic devotion
> she glorified her calling
> by sacrificing her own life
> that others might live.**

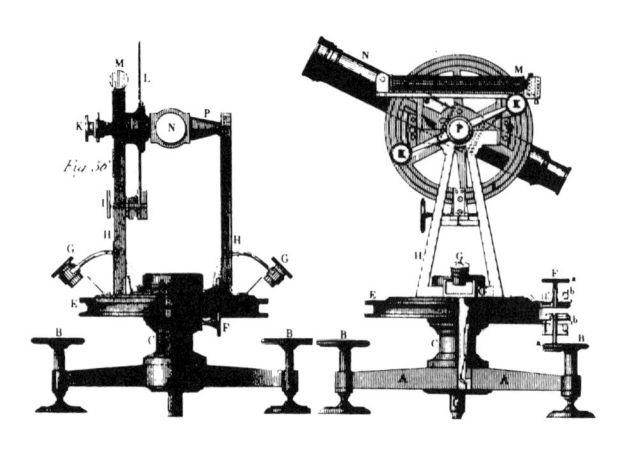

Sometimes an epitaph may be a bit confusing. We may not be sure if it says what the deceased would have wanted. Perhaps it was written by a living relative, playing a joke on the deceased. For example, the gravestone of Professor Joseph W. Holden, an astronomer, reads:

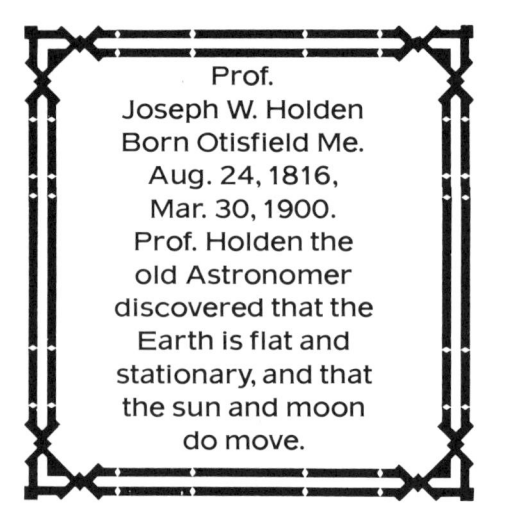

> **Prof.
> Joseph W. Holden
> Born Otisfield Me.
> Aug. 24, 1816,
> Mar. 30, 1900.
> Prof. Holden the
> old Astronomer
> discovered that the
> Earth is flat and
> stationary, and that
> the sun and moon
> do move.**

Other epitaphs leave no doubt about how the living felt about the deceased:

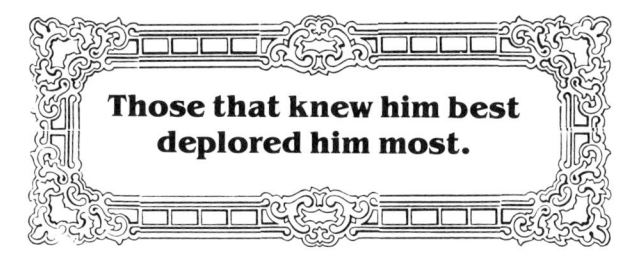

> **Those that knew him best deplored him most.**

Sometimes epitaphs are used to sum up the life of the deceased. The gravestone of H. Amenzo Dygert, who died at the age of 78 in 1924, tells that he was:

> **An American by birth**
> **A German Dutchman by descent**
> **A Republican in Politics**
> **A Congregationalist in Religion**
> **A Druggist by Profession**
> **A Bachelor by fate.**

In some cemeteries you may run across an epitaph that explains the source of a famous legend or part of American culture and history. In the Oakwood Cemetery in Troy, New York, the tomb of Samuel Wilson has this epitaph:

> U.S.
> In loving memory
> of
> "Uncle Sam"
> The name
> Originating with
> Samuel Wilson
> 1766-1854
> During the War of 1812
> And since adopted by
> The United States

Samuel Wilson was a meat packer. During the War of 1812, one of his shipments to Elbert Anderson was stamped "EAUS." The "EA" designated Mr. Anderson, the purchaser. The "US" designated the contractor, Uncle Sam, which was what Samuel Wilson's friends called him. It is said that even the soldiers from Troy recognized that the meat came from the meat packer Uncle Sam. So what began as a private joke in Troy, New York, became an important part of American culture. To this day, the figure of Uncle Sam is used to symbolize the United States government.

Too often in recent years we haven't taken the time or made the effort to leave messages like these on our tombstones. Compared to many of those you will find in older cemeteries, our gravestones today seem uninteresting and uncaring.

103

WRITING YOUR OWN EPITAPH

Many people, especially in the 1800s, wrote their own epitaphs long before they died. Or family or close friends may have composed an epitaph for the tombstone of a loved one.

In either case, the epitaph is a last chance to leave behind a message to the world. It can tell about your life or something you have done that was important. It might even be a sermon you want to leave behind for the living. It may be a sample of your sense of humor. An epitaph may also be in the form of a favorite poem or verse that says something about your philosophy or your life.

Write your own epitaph. Here is your chance to decide what sort of message you would like to leave to history. You may want to leave a bit of a mystery or perhaps a joke. Or maybe your epitaph will be very serious. Whatever you decide, also describe why you wrote what you did.

SYMBOLISM FOUND ON TOMBSTONES AND MONUMENTS

Perhaps as you have walked through a cemetery you have been tempted to touch some of the gravestones. You may have wanted to run your fingers over their designs and feel the type of stone they are carved from.

Tombstones and monuments are not just sources of historical information because of their dates and inscriptions. Their designs and the symbolism of their decorations are also part of the message left behind.

These decorations may have had special meaning because their symbolism expressed what the deceased wanted on his or her gravestone. Or they may have been chosen by loved ones to express something about the deceased, his or her life, or his or her attitude about death. They may have religious meaning. Or they may symbolize what the person did in his or her life. The decorations may also help us interpret the epitaph itself.

The decorations on tombstones and monuments may also be important because they were chosen by the carver to express his or her own sense of what is beautiful and what has meaning. Other times these designs may simply be decorations the carver chose to fill in empty spaces on the stone to make it more beautiful.

If you learn to decode the symbolism of the designs you find on tombstones, you will often be able to read the message without even reading the words of the epitaph. In fact, this was often the purpose of these decorations. They were meant to be understood even by people who couldn't understand the particular language the inscription was carved in.

Always remember that even though the symbolism and decorations of many old gravestones may seem strange to you, they were understood by the people who lived at the time the person died. Not only are these monuments sources of historical information but they are also artifacts of our past culture.

105

Head and footstone

Tomb

Almost all tombstones and monuments have some date on them and bear some sort of kinship data about the deceased person. Headstones are usually upright slabs of stone set over the grave. The main decoration is usually at the top of the headstone. The inscription is beneath the design. First the name, age, and dates of birth and death are given, and then the epitaph. The sides of the stone may also be decorated with geometric or floral designs. The footstone is a smaller stone placed at the other end of the grave.

Tablestones are flat, carved slabs of stone that are raised up on four, six, or eight legs. A tomb is usually a large, flat, carved slab placed over a large brick or stone base. Slabstones are large flat stones with carving on top that are placed flat against the ground.

Many early gravestones are decorated with symbols for the passing of time that show that life is short. These symbols include the hourglass or clock; old Father Time with a long beard; or a scythe. Sometimes the hourglass has wings because man is mortal and his hour on Earth is brief.

Tablestone

Symbols of the certainty of death include:

a death's head, usually with wings and blank eyes

a skull with crossbones

skeletons

arrows and darts

coffins

pickaxes and spades

crowing cock

These designs form a warning to the living that:

**Death is a debt to nature due
Which I have paid and so must you.**

Many other very old tombstones have symbols of the Resurrection and of the immortality of the soul. These include:

trumpets

rising suns

torches

an open Bible

winged cherubs

winged souls

angels

By the mid-1800s many other, less morbid symbols were being used by stonecarvers. An urn represented the container of the human life from which the soul rises to heaven.

The willow tree symbolized the sorrow of the end of a life on Earth and the joy of a life in heaven. Hands pointing upward, crowns, cherubs, and trees all were part of the symbolism for the glory of the soul's journey to an afterlife.

Arches were often used to represent the gateway to heaven. Broken pillars indicated that a life had been cut short. This symbolism was usually found on a child's gravestone, as were lambs. Sometimes larger tombs and mausoleums were built to represent Greek, Roman, and Gothic temples.

Sometimes the monument, sarcophagus, or headstone has a symbolic portrait of the deceased. They may be dressed in a uniform that tells what their occupation was. A coat-of-arms may be used to signify their heritage.

There may also be brass plates or seals on the stone that indicate that the person belonged to a certain fraternal organization or fought in a war. For example, you may find the following information on veterans' gravestones:

American Revolutionary War and the War of 1812 — stated inside a circular shield.

Civil War — G.A.R. stands for the Grand Army of the Republic or the Union Army while C.S.A. stands for the Confederate States Army.

Spanish American War — full cross with the date and name of the war surrounded by a list of the areas of action.

World War I — either the name of the war or an American Legion shield.

World War II — an eagle stating the name of the war.

SYMBOLISM IN THE CEMETERY

As you walk through a local cemetery make a chart of the symbolism you find on the gravestones, tombs, and monuments. If the cemetery is really large, pick a smaller section to study. You may trace or photocopy as many copies of the chart included in this book as you need.

List the symbols you come across and what you think they mean. Group the symbols as to whether they stand for time passing, the Resurrection, or perhaps the deceased person's occupation. Keep track of how many tombstones have each symbol. Be sure to list the age of each stone.

Also note whether the symbols agree with the epitaphs. Are certain symbols used more for a particular age group? Do women's graves seem to have different symbols than men's? Do the symbols seem to reflect specific religions or the ethnic background of the deceased?

Be sure to look for any information on who carved the stone. You may find the stonecutter's name or initials. Also check whether the stone includes any brass plaques or seals that tell you that the deceased belonged to a certain organization or fought in a war.

As you walk through the cemetery you will notice that decorations on headstones and monuments have changed over the years. Try to determine when certain designs were most popular. How does their popularity reflect other aspects of the culture at that time?

PRESERVING CEMETERIES AND THEIR HISTORY

As you have learned, cemeteries are one of our richest sources of historical and cultural information about communities and the people who have lived in them. The messages from the past found in cemeteries are not meant to be ignored. They should be treasured and preserved. Cemeteries are also places that may have important religious meanings for many people. Since they are the final resting place of our deceased family and friends, they may have strong emotional meaning for us.

Too many cemeteries in our country are neglected and forgotten. You may have even come across broken or missing stones in the cemeteries you have visited. If maintained and understood, a cemetery can contribute to the life of a community. A cemetery should be a place where you can go to pay homage to the dead. It can also be a laboratory for discovering all sorts of information about a town and its people. But the cemetery and its gravestones must be respected and kept up.

The information on gravestones that are worn or damaged may be preserved by photographing the stones. If the carving on the stone is in low-relief this may be very difficult to do. It is best to use Kodak Panatomic X film. Slow film is better because it can produce images of higher contrast. The light and shadow will bring up the texture and inscriptions on the stone. It is also best to take photographs in bright or filtered sun.

Another way to preserve the historical and cultural information found in a cemetery is to make rubbings of the gravestones or monuments. Many times a rubbing of a low-relief or worn inscription makes it possible to read lines that you can't decode on the stone itself.

HOW TO MAKE A RUBBING

Rubbing is a method of reproducing various carved, sculpted, engraved, cast, and natural surfaces. A piece of paper or cloth is placed on top of an object or surface. It is rubbed or dabbed with graphite, a wax crayon, or ink.

The easiest way to understand how a rubbing works is to make a very simple one. Place a coin underneath a sheet of white paper. Carefully rub the surface of the coin with a pencil until the figure's outline and form appear.

Rubbings have been used to make records of architecture and sculpture all over the world. They have been made of everything from sewer covers (which often include detailed decorations, manufacturing information, and dates) to the doors of churches.

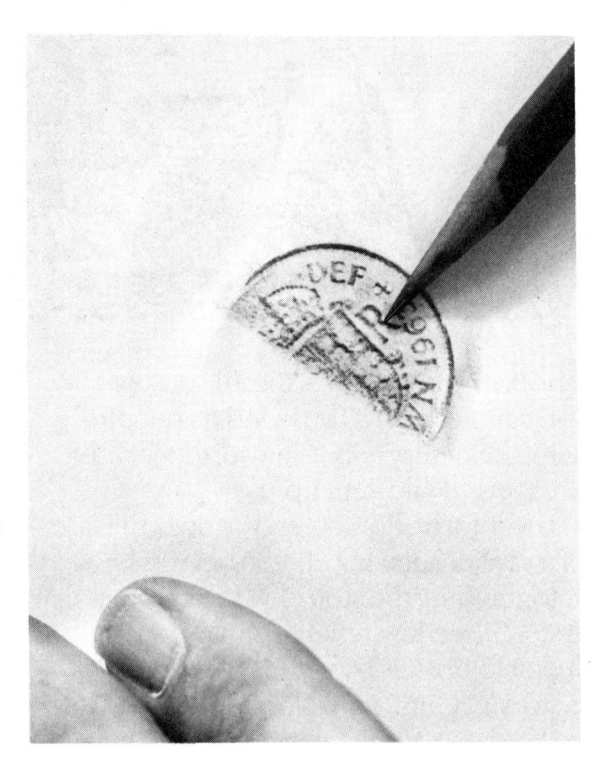

Permission should always be obtained to make a rubbing in a cemetery. As long as you are responsible and considerate, most places will not only cooperate but encourage you in your work.

Many different methods can be used to make a rubbing but the simplest requires the following materials:

roll of masking tape

large roll or pad of shelf lining paper, brown wrapping paper, newsprint paper, rice paper, or aquaba paper (made from hemp)

scissors

box of hard black wax crayons or rubbing waxes

All of these materials are usually available at art supply stores. Aquaba paper, which comes in rolls and sheets, is probably the best type of paper to make rubbings with.

Follow these steps in making a rubbing:

1. The first step in making a rubbing is to clean the object or surface being rubbed to remove dirt, lichen, and other particles.

2. Once the surface is clean, tape a piece of paper over it. Make sure that the paper cannot shift position. If it does, your design will come out blurred.

3. Rub the broad edge of a crayon over the entire surface of the gravestone or object. The general outlines of the design should begin to appear. The raised parts of the design will be black. The recessed parts will be white or the color of your paper.

4. Once you have established the overall design, go back and rub the undefined areas more firmly until the design becomes clearer. With a little bit of practice you should be able to make rubbings that are not only of historical interest but are also beautiful.

5. Always sign your rubbing with a pencil. Note the date and place where the rubbing was made. In this way, you will establish a record for future generations of who made the rubbing, when and where it was made, as well as identifying the gravestone message you have preserved.

— Durham, Connecticut

COLLECTING CEMETERY RUBBINGS

You can record the history, epitaphs, and art of your local cemetery by making a collection of gravestone rubbings.

Get permission from the cemetery near where you live and collect together all of the materials you will need to make a rubbing.

Decide which gravestones you want to make rubbings of. You may be interested in making a record of the stones that have become badly worn and are hard to read. You might want to collect examples of gravestone symbols and designs or epitaphs. You may even be lucky enough to be able to make a collection of rubbings from the tombstones of your own ancestors.

Be sure to sign your rubbings and write down on them when and where they were made so that you have a permanent historical record of messages from the past.

USEFUL TERMS IN STUDYING CEMETERIES

You may run across some words or abbreviations on gravestones that you do not know. Here is a list of common terms used both on gravestones and in talking about them.

AE: An abbreviation for Aetatis, or years of life.

ARTIFACT: An object made or shaped by human workmanship.

B.P.O.E.: Benevolent Protective Order of Elks, a fraternal organization.

CATACOMB: An underground network of chambers or tunnels with recesses in which to place the dead.

CEMETERY: A place for burying the dead; a graveyard.

COLUMBARIUM: A vault with niches for urns containing ashes of the dead.

CONSORT: A husband alive at the time of his wife's death.

C.S.A.: Confederate States Army.

D.S.P: (Latin — *decessit sine prole*) Died without issue (children).

D.V.P.: (Latin — *decessit vita patris*) Died in father's lifetime.

D.Y.: Died young.

EPITAPH: An inscription on a tombstone or monument in memory of the person or persons buried there. An epitaph is also a short statement in memory of a deceased person.

FOOTSTONE: A stone marking the foot of a grave.

G.A.R.: Grand Army of the Republic, or Union Army.

GRAVESTONE: A stone that marks a grave.

GRAVEYARD: An area set aside as a burial ground.

GRAVEYARD SHIFT: A work shift that runs during the early morning hours, such as from midnight to 8:00 a.m.

HEADSTONE: A memorial stone set at the head of a grave.

H.S.: (Latin — *hic situs or sepultus*) Here is buried.

I.H.S.: Greek spelling of "Christ."

INTER: To bury or put a dead body into a grave or tomb.

I.O.O.F.: Independent Order of Odd Fellows, a fraternal organization.

MAUSOLEUM: A large, stately tomb, or a building housing a tomb or tombs.

MEMORIAL: Something that is a reminder of some event or person, such as an arch, a column, a statue, or a holiday.

MONUMENT: A structure such as a building, arch, pillar, statue, tomb, or stone set up to honor a person or an event.

O.E.S.: Order of Eastern Star, an organization for women.

OBIT.: Died.

OBIT SINE PROLE: Died without children.

PLAT: A small piece of ground.

PLOT: A small piece of ground.

POTTER'S FIELD: A place where unknown or poor (destitute) persons are buried.

RELICT: A widow.

SARCOPHAGUS: A stone coffin, often ornamental. Sometimes the ancient Egyptians used a stone that was almost pure lime from a special region of Asia Minor to carve a sarcophagus. According to Pliny (A.D. 23-79), a Roman scholar and author, a sarcophagus made of the stone would completely destroy the body interred in it within forty days. Thus, its name is derived from two Greek words, *sarx*, meaning "flesh," and *phagos*, which means "eating."

SEPULCHER: A place of burial; a tomb; a grave.

TOMBSTONE: A stone or monument, inscribed, that marks a grave; a gravestone.

V.F.W.: Veterans of Foreign Wars.

SYMBOLISM IN THE CEMETERY CHART

Draw basic shape of tombstone:

Student name _____ Date _____

Name of cemetery _____

Location _____

Date founded _____

Founded by _____

Inscription _____
_____

Epitaph _____
_____

Plaque or seal _____

Type of stone used for tombstone _____

Age of tombstone _____

Information on carver of stone _____
_____

List of symbols and decorations _____
_____
_____

Sex of deceased _____

Age of death _____

Occupation _____

Religious/ethnic background _____

Economic status of deceased _____

Note on condition of tombstone _____

Location of tombstone in cemetery _____

Copyright © 1984 by Addison-Wesley Publishing Company

INVENTORY OF CEMETERIES CHART

Name of cemetery	Location	Public or private Religious/ethnic affiliation	Comments

CEMETERY CENSUS CHART

Name of cemetery _____

Location _____

Date founded _____

Founded by _____

Last name	First and middle names	Birthdate

Birthplace	Language of inscription	Ethnic origin of surname

Additional Credits
Photographs by
    Eugene F. Provenzo, Jr. 89, 92, 93, 94, 105, 107, 112
    Steven D. Freedman 106, 108, 111
    Peter A. Zorn, Jr. 110

Photographs from the family collection of
    Asterie Baker Provenzo 25, 28, 29, 30, 31, 32, 33, 66, 67, 72
    Eugene F. Provenzo, Jr. 60, 68, 71
    Julia Thrane Zorn 25, 30, 31
    Peter A. Zorn, Jr. 49, 84, 85
    Aubrey Simms 78

Documents and memorabilia from the family
collection of
    Asterie Baker Provenzo 32, 50, 79
    Eugene F. Provenzo, Jr. 52, 60, 61, 69, 70
    Peter A. Zorn, Jr. 65, 79, 85

Illustrations from Edmund Vincent Gillion, Jr.
Early New England Gravestone Rubbings
(New York: Dover Publications, Inc., 1966) 88, 96, 97, 98, 105, 107